To my wife, Page.

Special thanks to Booton Herndon, my collaborator,
for his professional expertise in the organization and presentation
of the text in this book.

Designed by Marilyn F. Appleby, with the assistance of A. Barclay Kraft.
Edited by Kathleen D. Valenzi, with the assistance of Lori L. Adkins.
Text copyright © 1989 by George H. Gilliam. All rights reserved.
Photography copyright © 1989 by Mark Meyer. All rights reserved.
This book, or any portions thereof, may not be reproduced or
transmitted in any form or by any means, electronic or mechanical,
including photocopying, recording, or by any information storage and
retrieval system, without permission in writing from the publisher.
Text may not be reproduced without permission of George H. Gilliam.
Photography may not be reproduced without permission of Mark Meyer.
Library of Congress Catalog Card Number 88-62456
ISBN 0-943231-18-3
Printed and bound in Hong Kong.
Published by Howell Press, Inc., 1147 River Road, Bay 2,
Charlottesville, Virginia 22901. Tel : (804) 977-4006.
Third Printing

HOWELL PRESS

RACIN'

THE NASCAR/WINSTON CUP STOCK CAR RACING SERIES

PHOTOGRAPHS BY MARK MEYER

TEXT BY GEORGE H. GILLIAM

C O N T E N T S

PREFACE	**17**
RACIN'	**22**
THE CARS	**41**
THE DRIVERS	**71**
Cale Yarborough	
Richard Petty	
Buddy Baker	
Bobby Allison	
Benny Parsons	
Darrell Waltrip	
Neil Bonnett	
Harry Gant	
Dale Earnhardt	
Ricky Rudd	
Sterling Marlin	
Bill Elliott	
Terry Labonte	
Geoff Bodine	
Alan Kulwicki	
Kyle Petty	
Rusty Wallace	
Rick Wilson	
Bobby Hillin Jr.	
Ken Schrader	
Davey Allison	
Brett Bodine	
NASCAR	**171**
BIG MONEY	**181**

PREFACE

For the past couple of years, I've lived a life any Winston Cup racing fan would exchange his tickets to the Daytona 500 for. I've not only been watching the races from the pit areas, I've ridden with Darrell Waltrip at Talladega as he explained how he drives that track. Sterling Marlin let me wear his crew's radio headphones at Daytona. I chatted with Bill Elliott in his trailer on a cold and wet day at Martinsville, and Bobby Hillin Jr. took me out to lunch. Buck Baker gave me special attention when I took the basic, three-day, Winston Cup course at his driving school at Rockingham, North Carolina, where I drove the high-banked, oval track myself. I ski fast and fly high-performance planes, but going into those turns at racing speed is something else. Dale Earnhardt shed his One Tough Guy image long enough to reveal that he is, underneath it all, one tough guy. I talked with a lot of drivers and found them to be as interesting standing still as they are whizzing around superspeedways at the rate of a football field per second. Jeff Hammond, Darrell Waltrip's crew chief, and Richard Childress, owner of Dale Earnhardt's car, each let me watch major races from their pit areas and explained race strategy to me as the competition progressed.

I have visited a number of the shops where the cars are made and talked with the owners, engine builders, and other craftsmen who are responsible for them. Junior Johnson showed me around his state-of-the-art shops in the Brushy Mountains of North Carolina, bordered by a corn field, a chicken house with 160,000 residents ("I've got a lot of mouths to feed"), a coon-dog run, and a helicopter pad. Richard Childress spent several hours showing me how he and Kirk Shelmerdine's crew built the cars and Lou LaRosa built the engines that won the 1986 and 1987 Winston Cup Championships. Jimmy Johnson, overseer of the three-car, Hendrick Motorsports stable, walked me through his operations, and Waddell Wilson patiently explained how a race engine is prepared. Owner of three of the top teams in the sport, Rick Hendrick, the automobile mega-dealer from Charlotte, North Carolina, described his vision of the future of stock car racing.

The top-gun drivers and powerful racing machines would go blasting out into space if it were not for NASCAR keeping their feet and wheels on the ground. Bill France, the founder of modern stock car racing; his son Bill Jr., who has brought racing into the age of television coverage and multimillion-dollar sponsorships; and all the officials

of NASCAR have opened their doors for me. Jim Hunter, a sportswriter who used to sleep on the floor of Cale Yarborough's motel room to save money, now Vice President for Administration; Jim Foster, NASCAR's marketing whiz; Bob Weeks, Director of Sponsor Services; and Les Richter, Vice President for Competition, have each spent hours helping me to understand the intricacies of the racing establishment.

This exciting time began for me a number of years ago when a friend, Jerry Baliles, now Governor of Virginia, asked me to attend a Winston Cup race with him. Had it been anyone else, I probably would have begged off. Like many other people, I thought stock car racing was only for rednecks with gun racks in their pickup trucks. At that first race I was surprised at how many prosperous-looking *families* were present in an atmosphere that rivals Disney World for exuberance. When the race began and the brightly colored cars surged forward with an incredible roar of acceleration, I was hooked. My wife started attending the races with me, and her fascination with the sport helped me understand why 38 percent—and growing—of the spectators are women.

I wanted to learn more about the sport. I wanted to know something about the drivers and how the cars were built. I wanted to know what NASCAR was all about and why major national corporations have gone so wild with sponsorships for race cars. I went to bookstores and libraries looking for books; though I came up with autobiographies of Cale Yarborough and Richard Petty, I did not find what I was looking for.

So I decided to write the book I wanted to buy. As a lawyer who drafts contracts and other legal documents, I have a hard time writing a sentence without adding at least two "Whereases" in it. A friend and professional writer, Booton Herndon, agreed to help. Finally, the superbly talented Mark Meyer of *Time* Magazine, who photographed jets for *Wings* and warbirds for *Classics: U.S. Aircraft of World War II*, agreed to take the photographs for this book, which also features things that are made out of metal and go fast.

We have had a good time living out the dreams of many race fans. I hope you enjoy reading this book and looking at the pictures as much as we have enjoyed producing it.

Charlottesville, Virginia, July, 1988.

R A C I N '

It was a hot Sunday afternoon in September 1987. Heat was shimmering off the tight, 0.542-mile asphalt track at Richmond Fairgrounds Speedway in Virginia's capital city. Forty thousand fans were packed into the grandstands surrounding the track and in the infield area of the oval. They breathed in the fumes of engine exhaust and burned rubber as the roar of 32 unmuffled race cars, each running a 650-horsepower engine at 7,500 rpm, assaulted their ears. The race was in the 316th lap, 84 to go. Dale Earnhardt, driver of the yellow-and-blue Chevrolet Monte Carlo SS, car Number 3 sponsored by Wrangler Jeans, was leading. Darrell Waltrip, driving the orange-red-and-yellow Chevrolet, car Number 17 sponsored by Tide, was third.

The second-place car "got loose"—the rear end slid to the right in the corners—and Waltrip brought the Tide machine down low, inside the oval, and passed it. Now it was Earnhardt-Waltrip, one-two. Everybody at the track knew a classic confrontation was underway.

Actually, this car-to-car combat between two of the greatest drivers in racing had been going on for years. At this very track a year and a half before in February 1986, the Earnhardt car and the Waltrip car had tangled hard. Near the end of the race with Waltrip leading, Earnhardt's car ran into Waltrip's on the backstretch. Both spun and hit the wall. Another car sped by the two bashed-up combatants and won the race. Furious at what he and most observers thought was an intentional and unnecessary wrecking of his $60,000 race car, Waltrip drove the mangled car, sheet metal sticking out, around the track, sought out Earnhardt, and deliberately rammed him.

Waltrip and Earnhardt are natural adversaries, made to order for racing. Earnhardt, nicknamed "Ironhead" by some drivers, is known as *aggressive* in a sport where only the most aggressive even make it onto the track. His 1987 sponsor, Wrangler Jeans, encouraged his One Tough Customer image to market their rugged product. In the pits where most crews wear white uniforms, Earnhardt's crew wore blue so dark that it evoked images of Darth Vader.

If Earnhardt is One Tough Customer, Darrell Waltrip

is the White Knight. Known in his youth as mouthy and arrogant, Waltrip has become clean-cut, mature, and articulate. Sponsored by Proctor and Gamble's Tide detergent and by Exxon Corporation's Superflo Oils, Waltrip's image is squeaky-clean, the darling of the homemaker and big corporate America.

Though he did not say so, NASCAR/Winston Cup Director Dick Beaty surely had these drivers in mind at the pre-race meeting on this hot 1987 September Sunday in Richmond. Beaty warned that any driver guilty of "hotheaded behavior" would be black-flagged off the track for a cooling-off period. This is one of the most severe penalties NASCAR can impose, and Waltrip and Earnhardt were slapped with it before the race was halfway over. At lap 182 during a yellow-flag caution period, both drivers went to the pits for gas and tires. On pit road, crowded with cars being refueled and tires being changed and crew members dancing around the cars, the two bumped into each other. Though each blamed the other, NASCAR officials on the scene were immediately responsive to this unusual and dangerous action. They black-flagged both drivers and sent them to the back of the 32-car field.

But no NASCAR black flag could dull Waltrip and Earnhardt's superb driving skills or slow their stout racing machines. By lap 245 Earnhardt and Waltrip had worked their way back to the front of the lead lap. All through the crowd the tension was building. At lap 317 Earnhardt and Waltrip were one-two. Fans rose from their seats in the grandstand. The other cars on the track seemed to give space to the two leaders, knights in armor fighting it out on the track.

Richmond is the ideal track for such a confrontation. At the superspeedways, longer tracks where speed can build up to 200 miles per hour, there is little contact between the cars. It is just too dangerous at those speeds. But on the short tracks, green-flag lap speeds run just under 100 miles per hour. There is minimal banking, so the cars tend to slide to the outside in the tight turns. The turns are narrow, making it almost impossible for two cars to negotiate the same corner without touching. There's a lot of rubbing and exchanging of paint, but at the slower speeds seldom is anyone seriously hurt. The cars themselves bear extra reinforcement under their sheet metal skins in order to withstand the punishment.

Now it was lap 350 and Earnhardt and Waltrip were still one-two. As the race wore on, the tires on each car were getting slicker, making it harder to get any bite in the corners. Waltrip knew it was almost impossible for either to muster the acceleration necessary to pass the other. Yet lap after lap, turn after turn, he kept trying. He pushed the snout of his car down low under Earnhardt in the turns, his right front fender rubbing Earnhardt's left rear quarter panel. Earnhardt—with gifted eye-hand coordination and driving skills honed by hundreds of races on short tracks—would hold his line and step on the gas coming out of the corners, not letting Waltrip nudge him aside or get ahead.

"I couldn't run on the bottom, and I was slipping and sliding down there," Earnhardt said after the race. "But I could run more consistently up top, and that's the reason I beat him off the corners."

Waltrip had trouble getting the bite he needed. "I could get no traction off the turns," he commented. "I couldn't grip it the way I wanted. I would hit the gas and spin the tires."

In racing, the few consistent winners push their cars just beyond the absolute edge and hang on to win. Those with less courage either do not get quite to the edge or fail to hang on if they do. On the other hand, those with less skill, experience, or sensitivity go too far beyond the edge and crash.

Now, in Waltrip's case, the speed of that absolute edge was reduced by his worn tires. In every turn, just as he started to push ahead, Waltrip had to "feather the throttle" just a bit to avoid sliding. Earnhardt would then jump past him again. As Waltrip later observed, "On short tracks, if you want to win, you've got to go into the corner second and come out first." He was going into the corners second or sometimes even but coming out second by two or three feet.

More laps, more turns, more tension in the stands. Fans forgot about the other drivers. At this race in the closing laps, you were either a Waltrip fan or an Earnhardt fan. Viewing this race-within-a-race, this man-to-man combat between two of the outstanding drivers of the era, all you could do was slap the nearest back and yell, "That's racin'!"

Waltrip kept on pushing up underneath; Earnhardt continued to beat him out of the corners. Several times Waltrip edged a few feet past Earnhardt on the short back straightaway, but Earnhardt, who was running high on the corners, regained the lead. Earnhardt said of Waltrip, "He was stronger than me several times during the race, and if he could have gotten by me, I don't think I could have gotten it back."

With two laps to go, Waltrip knew he had only one way to win. He made his plans for the last lap. On turns one and two, he'd get under Earnhardt, hold on, and run alongside him. Then he'd go into turn three hard, all out. Instead of backing off the accelerator, he'd hold it down. If the car started to slide, maybe it would slide into Earnhardt and nudge him out of the way. But if it spun out of control? If he lost it altogether? Well, that's what makes car races.

Nevertheless, the best-laid plans of mice, men, and Darrell Waltrip do sometimes fail. While he was planning his strategy, running door-handle to door-handle with Earnhardt on the backstretch, his plans were dashed by something that happened on another part of the track. Neil Bonnett ground-looped his Pontiac and crashed. Yellow flag. No passing. Waltrip was one lap shy of giving it his last shot.

The race was over—but nobody left the stands. On the cool-down lap, Waltrip came up to run side by side with Earnhardt. Bitter contestants just minutes before, they now waved at each other and to the crowd. The crowd— which had booed one or the other driver during the pre-race introductions—now cheered them both. And off the track on pit road, something happened that may never have happened before but perhaps now will happen again. Out of the pits came the Waltrip and Earnhardt crews. Spontaneously, without direction, they formed two moving lines. Each man shook hands with every member of the opposite crew, expressing admiration and respect.

Earnhardt earned $44,950 in victory; Waltrip pocketed $22,680 for second place. Neither had wrecked the other's car or his own. It had been a real race.

—

Twenty-nine NASCAR-sanctioned races are run each year on the Winston Cup Circuit, the major league of stock car racing. It's named for the cigarette made by the R.J. Reynolds Tobacco Company, which annually contributes several million dollars to the sport. The races are run on 15 tracks in 12 states, from New York to California, from Michigan to Alabama. Lengths of the tracks range from 0.526 miles at the Martinsville Speedway in Virginia, where lap speeds are in the 80s, to the 2.66-mile track of the Alabama International Speedway at Talladega, where lap

speeds have exceeded 214 miles per hour. All but two races are run counterclockwise on oval tracks. The road courses at the 2.42-mile Watkins Glen track in New York and the 2.62-mile Riverside, California, track (razed to make way for a development in 1988) demand both left and right turns. At the short tracks—those less than a mile long—races are run for 400 or 500 laps—200 to 250 miles; at the longer tracks, races are run twice as far—500 or 600 miles on 2 to 2 1/2-mile ovals. More than 2,300,000 spectators attend Winston Cup races annually (twice the number that watch Indy cars), buying tickets that cost as much as Broadway musicals. A hundred million more watch telecasts on CBS, ABC, and ESPN. Auto racing is the nation's third most attended sport—behind baseball and horse racing, ahead of professional football and basketball.

When cars are pushed out onto the track by their teams, they look like the Chevrolets, Fords, Buicks, Oldsmobiles, and Pontiacs you see in your dealer's showroom. In fact these are custom-made machines with little more than the engine block and the sheet metal skin conforming to the manufacturer's stock. Though each car appears to be identical from track to track, under the hood and body are actually motors and chassis, brakes and suspension systems specifically designed for use at short tracks, superspeedways, or left-right road courses. All in all, these cars are designed by the best engineering minds in the business, hand-built by the last of the true custom craftsmen, and driven by the best athletes in the sport.

In the early days of racing, drivers drove their cars to the track. The first race at Darlington, South Carolina, in 1950 was won by a car bought off the showroom floor. It was as recent as the mid-1950s that Lee Petty was the talk of the track for transporting his car to the race on a flatbed trailer. Petty added to the drama by covering the car with a canvas tarpaulin emblazoned with his racing colors. Now, even the mid-ranked teams arrive at tracks with two race-ready cars packed piggyback in custom-made Komfort Koach trailers featuring hydraulic lifts and pulled by Peterbilt cabs with velour seats.

Crews come in several days before a race. Most teams keep a detailed book on each racecourse and set up their cars by adjusting the chassis at the home shop and then making final adjustments at the tracks. The extra car is left on the truck unless something happens to the primary car before the race; unloading it costs another entry fee. When the cars are ready, the drivers arrive, usually in private planes, for practice. They run several laps in which they accelerate to race speeds. At the pits Goodyear and Hoosier tire engineers are waiting with probing thermometers to take tire temperatures. From this they can determine how well the four tires are sticking to the racing surface and consequently how well the car is set up for the track.

No matter how good a record a team may keep on each track, minor adjustments are almost always necessary. Racing surfaces vary not only from track to track but from race to race, day to day, and even hour to hour. If rain washes away the minute particles of rubber left over from the last race, for example, the surface changes. An overcast day means lower temperatures on the asphalt, demanding one type of setup to achieve peak adhesion. If the clouds lift and the sun beats down, an altogether different tire and chassis setup may be required. The tires and setup that worked last year, or yesterday, or five minutes ago, may not be right now. Crews continually strive for perfect adhesion in order to make the cars grip, as Darrell Waltrip puts it, "like cats wearing sneakers."

In their practice runs the drivers explore the track. On every curve on every track, there is a precise lane for every car at every speed. It is called the "groove." Alone on the track, each driver seeks his groove.

Two days before the race, the drivers begin running in small groups, feeling how their cars react to the aerodynamics of other cars. Each fast-moving car pushes air up and to the sides. Other cars thus encounter pockets of smooth air, pockets of turbulence, and, some claim, even areas of vacuum pressure behind and around the car. On the left and on the right, on straightaways and in turns, high and low on the track, drivers study what happens as they come up from behind and pass the car or cars ahead.

Sixty or more teams show up for the race but only 32 or 40, depending on the track, will race on Sunday. Qualifying runs determine who those teams will be and also set the starting position of those who make the field. The fastest qualifying cars start the race at the front of the pack. They won't have to fight their way through traffic to get ahead of the mob. Some drivers, like Dale Earnhardt, are extremely adept at moving from the rear to the front, threading their way among 30 or 40 cars traveling close together at high speed. Others, like Bill Elliott, run at their best when they start on the front row, get ahead of the pack, and stay

there. For those drivers who have trouble fighting their way up from the back of the pack, how well they do in qualifying may mean how well they do in the race.

Qualifying is a race in itself and altogether different from the main event. While the race proper lasts three or more hours and requires an engine that can run at sustained high rpm, qualifying races last only a minute or so and durability is not important.

NASCAR permits the use of different engines in qualifying and in the race, and each engine is driven differently. Although a car develops more horsepower with cooler operating temperatures, most teams when qualifying close off the front air ducts in order to force air over the car, rather than through the engine, for a cleaner aerodynamic line. If they tried that in a race, they'd burn out the engine in a hurry. In qualifying runs the driver is alone on the track and can stay in his own groove, so his crew sets up his chassis especially for that groove.

At most tracks qualifying boils down to one lap. The driver blasts out of the pit road and accelerates for a complete circuit. When he hits the electronic timing device at the starting line to begin the second lap, he has achieved maximum speed without overheating tires or engine. For this single qualifying lap, he "stands on it"—mashes the accelerator to the floor.

With your back to the track, you can almost tell from the sound of the engine how well a driver is going to qualify. The also-rans back off just a smidgen in the turns. With drivers who place in the top 20, it's one continuous, all-out roar. Sometimes, pushing the car to the absolute limit, a driver goes too far, loses control, and crashes all alone on the track. It may seem strange that a driver will risk his car and his neck racing against time, but that's how important qualifying is. After he has run his lap, he doesn't know how well he did until all the times are posted. The driver with the fastest time wins money and the "pole position" —an old horse-racing term meaning that he will start the race first in line with the inside track. Number two will be on his right in the double file, number three right behind him, number four behind number two, and so on.

Those who did not make the cut go home, leaving the track to those who did. Nineteen out of 20 repeat from race to race. Now the crews go back and start all over again, taking out the qualifying engine, putting in the race engine, adjusting the car for competition. A car practices an hour in the morning, another in the afternoon. Drivers wheel the cars out onto the track, run several laps, squeal back into the pits for tire temperature checks and chassis adjustments, then hurtle back for a few more laps.

Many tracks stage lower-division races on Saturday. These cars lay down enough rubber, which becomes embedded in the track unless it rains, to affect the surface for the Winston Cup race on Sunday. Saturday's setup may be all wrong for Sunday. Even if there is no change in track conditions, no reason to change the setup, there are thousands of moving parts in a car and engine, and pit crews keep on checking and tinkering and adjusting, striving for perfection. That's when the driver says, "It's runnin' real good."

Sunday starts early for both drivers and crew members. Old-timers tell of racers who partied all Saturday night and were poured bleary-eyed into their cars Sunday at noon. Not today. With millions invested and millions to win—and millions watching—drivers and crew members alike must be in superb physical and mental condition, well-rested and alert. A driver may drink a beer or two during the early part of the week, but he makes sure he keeps his edge as the race gets closer. As for drugs, NASCAR has a policy that requires drivers to submit to tests upon "reasonable suspicion." A driver testing positive is banned until he tests negative.

The crew chiefs—the head coaches of the operation—keep their pit crews testing and checking all morning. They've been known to replace an engine minutes before a race. Drivers, meanwhile, try to relax and stay loose. Two hours before the race is scheduled to begin, they change into their racing gear: soft racing shoes; Nomex suits, originally developed by NASA engineers after three astronauts perished in a launching-pad fire, which offer protection in the event of a gasoline fire for up to 12 minutes; and "cool suits," which are used in hot weather and contain piping through which coolant circulates.

A banner over the garage area announces:

WORSHIP SERVICE
HERE 11:00

A Southern Baptist preacher, Bill Baird, has established a ministry for those who cannot attend their home church during the 29-event race season, and most of the drivers, wives, and crew members attend. Darrell Waltrip, superstar driver with matinee-idol good looks, is active in this ministry. He stands with his arms wrapped around his wife Stevie and their baby Jessica Leigh. Ricky Rudd quietly holds hands with his blonde wife Linda. Even Richard Petty, the king of racing, bows his head—though he does not remove his elaborate black Stetson.

Dick Beaty, Winston Cup director, marshals his corps of NASCAR officials for the pre-race inspection. The cars are pushed through the inspection lanes. Each one must weigh at least 3,500 pounds. They can be unbalanced, with less weight on the outside, but the minimum right-side weight is 1,600 pounds. Tires are checked: one specific compound is legal on the right side of the car, another legal on the left. Templates conforming to the profile of the actual automobile model made in Detroit are passed over the cars to make sure their profiles are indeed that of a stock car. Once, before templates were in use, one winning car looked just like the showroom model but was discovered to be only seven-eighths size. Safety features required by NASCAR are checked: double shoulder straps, lap and groin belts, all securely anchored to the frame; front safety glass and rear plastic braced with at least three (two on short tracks) steel straps fastened to the frame. Carburetors are pulled apart and checked. At Daytona and Talladega the fastest cars used to go more than 210 miles per hour on the long laps; today NASCAR requires a restrictor plate in the carburetor that cuts top speeds down to the 190s. Cars that are deficient are sent back to their garages for remedial work. If a car is found to contain an illegal engine or other major component, it is disqualified, and the driver is suspended for 12 weeks.

An hour before race time, the drivers gather for the owner/driver meeting with NASCAR officials. Any tardy driver must start the race at the back of the pack, regardless of what position he has earned in the qualifying run. Dick Beaty calls the roll of drivers and car owners and, after all are accounted for, begins, "All right, you rednecks!" Everyone laughs, for this high-tech competition is no longer the exclusive turf of good ol' country boys. He reminds the drivers of the length of the race, and in his high-pitched, firm voice, he recites the race rules:

"At the start, you must cross the start/finish line before passing anyone or getting out of line. Violators will be black-flagged off the track. As soon as a caution flag appears, slow down. Do not drive close to the rescue crews and scare them; they are there to help you. If you hit the wall, you must go to the medical center to be checked. Under a yellow flag, only cars that are a lap or more down if they so desire may race the leader back to the start/finish line to unlap themselves. Do not pull out in front of the leader to block him.

"If you should spin, you lock her down, turn to the left, keep the brakes on, and come to a complete stop. Put the car in first gear, and drive to the pits for a set of tires. Under a yellow flag, the leaders may pit on the first lap, but if you're down one or more laps, we request you pit on the second yellow-flag lap so the pit road will not be so congested. When there is one remaining lap under yellow when the caution car turns off its flashing yellow lights, leaders go to the outside lane; those cars down one or more laps go to the inside lane. All passing regardless of lane is to the right-hand side.

"Do not jump the flag. We will keep a videotape of all action on pit road. If you see smoke, anticipate trouble and slow down. Know where the driver behind you is at all times. Fuel samples will be taken from all cars after the race; anyone found using any additive will be suspended for 12 weeks. Five cars will be taken down, disassembled and checked for compliance with NASCAR rules after the race. Slower cars should not run side by side; if you're caught in the middle lane, stay put, and let the faster cars pass you. Potential sponsors are in the stands, so give them a clean race.

"Gentlemen, have a safe race."

The drivers file out and walk toward their cars. Crews have pushed the cars into position in the order of the starting lineup on pit road. They remove the steering wheels so the drivers can climb in through the windows. There are no doors. They buckle themselves into their custom-made, ButlerBuilt seats, which wrap around the driver's right side to give extra support against the centrifugal force of the turns. They replace their steering wheels, which come up under their chins, and insert a holding pin. They put in their ear plugs and put on their helmets. The helmets contain earphones and microphones for two-way communication with the crew chief and are fastened by short restraining straps to the frame of the car. In a violent crash, these tethers take some strain off the driver's neck, and keep his head from being snapped forward or sideways.

NASCAR officials move crew members off the pit road. The Grand Marshal, usually the president of the corporation sponsoring the race, intones the traditional "Gentlemen, start your engines." The roar sounds like the end of the world, and fans hastily reach for their noise hushers, cushioned earphones that muffle the 120-decibel sound of the cars. The earphones protect against ear damage, but also have built-in radios to monitor Motor Racing Network's broadcast, with its frequent updates on car position.

The pace car leads the double-file line of cars around the track for three laps, picking up speed as the engines warm up. The drivers swerve from side to side to scuff and heat their tires. On the third lap the pace-car driver—acting on instructions from NASCAR officials in the control tower high above the track—cuts off the flashing yellow lights on top of his car. He rounds turn four, to the left of the start/finish line, and pulls off onto pit road. The double line of cars surges forward. By the time they reach the start/finish line, they are at full speed. On a superspeedway they will be traveling at more than 150 miles per hour; on a short track, around 90 miles per hour. The flagman, suspended in a basket over the track, drops the green flag. All over the stands fans say those spine-tingling words, "They're racin'!"

The front-running racers immediately put distance between themselves and the other cars. They find their groove and keep the throttle to the floor. Every driver has an immediate incentive to pass the leader, because if he leads for just one lap during the race, he earns five bonus points toward the Winston Cup point championship. The driver who leads the most laps earns five more. These points mean money at the Winston Cup Victory Dinner at the Waldorf-Astoria Hotel in New York City at season's end. As each driver tries to pass the car immediately ahead of him, the overall event breaks down into individual contests all over the track. When a car is hot on the tail of another, fans nudge each other and say, "They're racin'!" "Darrell is racin' Dale." "Bobby is racin' Richard."

Art experts know that a masterpiece is made up of hundreds of individual brush strokes; experienced race fans know a good race is made up of hundreds of individual contests. Sometimes the four or five leaders may be simply maintaining position with no action at the front of the pack, but a sudden roar will come from the crowd when they see two cars well back in the pack begin to jockey for position. Often the battle for ninth place is more intense, exciting,

and personal than the race for the lead.

NASCAR officials with two-way radios constantly monitor the race. They report to the tower, where senior NASCAR officials Dick Beaty and Les Richter watch the whole track. Suppose a car begins to leak oil, creating a hazard on the track. "Black flag Number 33!" Richter shouts. "Show the yellow." The flagman immediately waves the black flag at the offending driver, meaning "return to your pit for repairs." When the yellow flag goes up, yellow lights go on all around the track so that every driver, regardless of location, knows something is wrong. The cars race to the finish line to maintain position, then slow down immediately. The number of the leading car is radioed to the pace car—now the caution car—and it pulls onto the track in front of the leader just beyond the start/finish line. In this situation, under "caution" or "yellow," no car may pass another, except that a car which is a lap or more down may race the leader back to the start/finish line in an effort to regain the lost lap. Held back by the pace car, the procession winds slowly around the track until the track crews clean up the problem. The relaxed pace may actually be more than 100 miles per hour. Racing engines aren't made to run slow.

Though nothing seems to be happening, many races are won or lost under yellow. When some cars make pit stops, others keep going, increasing their lead or catching up. Here is where strategy enters, with crew chiefs making the vital decisions whether and when to bring in their cars for tires, fuel, and chassis adjustments.

The race is not won only on the track. While the spectators are cheering their heroes muscling their machines around the turns, the unsung members of the pit-crew teams are carrying on their own competition. A race car driver has to stop for gas, just like everybody else. The question is when. Each car can hold 22 gallons of fuel and averages four to five miles per gallon. On a 2.5-mile superspeedway, a car can make about 40 laps before refueling; on a short track, the cars can run as many as 200 laps. In today's high-tech world, computers figure it down to the last shot-glass full, but it still takes a human to decide the strategic moment to refill.

They've also got to change the tires. The life of treadless racing tires depends on the surface of the track, the temperature, and the setup of the car. Left-hand turns wear out right-side tires first, so they must be changed first. Again, the question is when. Squeeze the last millimeter of rubber out of them and risk a blowout? Or play it conservative and lose a lap to the car that stayed on the track?

Since the pit crews can't see much of the race, teams have a spotter in the stands with binoculars and a two-way radio looking out over the entire track to see when a car is leaking oil, pushing in the corners, or behaving in any way that requires chassis adjustments or instructions to the driver. In a 500-mile race in the summer at a superspeedway, the temperature in a car can reach plus-150 degrees. The pedals burn the driver's feet. After wrestling a wheel in exhaust fumes for three hours or more, a driver gets tired and drowsy. His voice reveals his condition. If a driver is overcome by heat or fumes, the rules permit him to be replaced.

Whatever all these factors—driver, fuel, tires, chassis, caution period—may total, at some point the crew chief has to bite the bullet and bring his driver in for a pit stop. Here another show within a show takes place. When the car lurches to a stop at its location on pit road, the six-man crew jumps over the wall and goes to work. They dump in up to 22 gallons of gas; they change two or four tires; and they do it in seconds.

Most races are won by less than five seconds, many by less than one; the crew that can change tires and add fuel in 14 seconds is more likely to be standing in Victory Lane at the end of the race than a crew taking 16 or 17 seconds. Some crew members are full-time, others are volunteer Sunday soldiers or weekend warriors who come only to work the races. As in dance routines or football and basketball plays, the pit routine is designed and rehearsed. Executed by six strong and skilled technicians in bright team uniforms emblazoned with the sponsor's logo, the tire-changing/refueling sequence has a distinct grace and beauty—though those may not be the words to use in front of the participants.

One man, handling a 50-pound jack like a toy, lifts one side of the car. Front- and rear-tire specialists hit the lugs with air guns, remove their wheels, replace them with new rubber carried by the fourth man. Lugs for the fresh tire are glued in place on the wheel. Before someone thought of gluing them on, the tire technician stored the new lugs in his mouth to have them ready. The crew chief dives through the window behind the driver, legs sticking out like a frog, and loosens or tightens wedge bolts to adjust the chassis. The fuel man forces Unocal 76 racing gasoline out of two 11-gallon cans into the fuel cell. Thanks to two-inch nozzles, vents in the tank, and his own skill, he can do it in less than 15 seconds.

Nobody wastes time with words or signals. When the person operating the jack sees that all crew members have finished their jobs, he drops the car. When the driver feels it hit the road, he guns it.

Sometimes it does not go all that smoothly. At Daytona in 1987 an air wrench belonging to Davey Allison's crew jammed. The tire technician moved away to get a new wrench. The man with the jack saw him turn and dropped the car. Allison took off and so did the wheel. A TV commentator punned, "You picked a fine time to leave me, loose wheel."

After the car moves out, the crew measures how much fuel was put in, computes the mileage the car is getting on that track on that day, and determines how many laps can be run before the next stop.

When the leader pits, another driver takes his place at the front of the pack. During caution periods when several front-runners make stops, the back-markers grab the lead for a few laps and several dollars. When the green flag restarts the race, however, the former leaders usually win their positions back in a few laps, particularly when those who stayed on the track have to go in themselves.

With all this going on, cars all over the track, some having lapped others more than once, how in the world do you know who's ahead of whom? The answer: Morris Metcalfe, chief NASCAR scorer, tells you.

Not too long ago, a group of volunteers, frequently the drivers' wives, kept score by taking a pebble out of one box and putting it in another each time her assigned car went by. Sometimes she might do it between times if nobody was looking. Today Metcalfe assigns two scorers to each car. Each team provides one scorer, NASCAR the rest. The NASCAR group is composed of volunteers, some of whom come in from hundreds of miles away. Their reward is the worst seat in the house, for they can see only a small portion of the track on either side of the start/finish line.

Each scorer has a sheet of paper printed on one side with hundreds of small blocks, one for each lap of the race. On the reverse side of the paper is printed, in large block, the number of the assigned car. Each time his or her car crosses the start/finish line, the scorer checks the official clock and notes the time of passage in the appropriate block. When the car completes 10 laps, the scorer holds up the pad so that Louise Frazier, a volunteer NASCAR official at the back of the room, can see it. She records the order of each car at 10-lap intervals and notifies the press booth and the NASCAR tower as to who's ahead. NASCAR is working on computers to improve the procedure but vows it will never eliminate the volunteer scorers.

This happy little group working conscientiously for nothing means millions of dollars to the race teams. The allocation of prize money for laps is an important factor in modern stock car racing. Once it was winner-take-all, which meant zip for everybody else. Today, the top teams stay in for the points that are earned by completing laps, even when something goes wrong in a race and there's no chance of winning.

But racers come to win, not simply to pile up points. Towards the end of the race when things get hairy, they take wild chances to win. In a race with few caution flags, particularly in the last 10 laps, they gamble on gas and tires. A driver may figure that even if he pits under a green flag and thus loses 15 or more seconds, with fresh tires he'll catch and pass cars that have 70 or 80 laps on theirs. As for gas, a driver who has been getting 80 laps to the tank may think he can stretch that to 85 laps and stay out on the track while the leader comes in. Long-time analysts of the sport say that the tire gamblers give up too much time to catch up. Benny Parsons, a senior driver, says fuel gambles work only two out of 10 times. As a compromise, teams have perfected a gas-and-go technique in which the gas man sloshes in two or three gallons on the run.

A NASCAR race is one you don't want to leave early. Even after the flagman waves the white flag to signal the beginning of the last lap, the race isn't over until it's over. Tanks run dry. Engines which have gone 499 miles at top speed can't make the 500th. Drivers running door handle to door handle bump each other in a final violent effort and wipe out both cars as well as whoever's behind. Finally the checkered flag falls. The winner goes to Victory Lane and gets a kiss from Miss Winston and warm embraces from his crew.

Everyone else goes home.

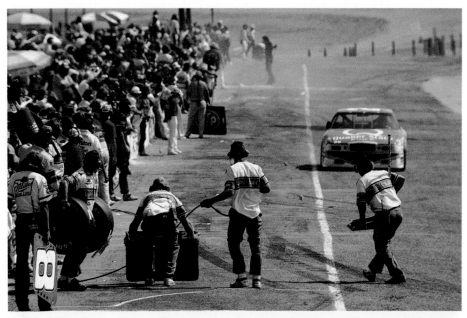

Pit stop, Riverside, California. On road courses, where cars travel clockwise, the fuel filler neck is located on the right-hand side of the car; on counterclockwise-traveled oval tracks, the neck is positioned on the left.

Rusty Wallace.

Goodwrer

T H E ■ C A R S

They are custom-made racers, hand-crafted by the most highly skilled builders of engine and car bodies in America. Each race car—which has the identical silhouette of its counterpart in your neighborhood showroom—costs upwards of $60,000. Only the sheet metal skin and engine block come from the factory.

In the beginning they were in fact stock cars. Ransom Olds raced his Olds Pirate to a 57-mile-per-hour tie with Alexander Winton's Bullet in 1902 before a crowd of 50 spectators on the beach at Ormond, just north of Daytona, Florida. Henry Ford raced the cars with his name on the hood, and William K. Vanderbilt raced the Mercedes he bought. Eddie Rickenbacker, America's greatest World War I ace and founder of Eastern Air Lines, was once a car dealer who raced his cars on dirt tracks. The car that won on Sunday sold on Monday.

Even after World War II, when organized stock car racing was in its infancy, "strictly stock" was the rule. Dealers drove their cars to the tracks, picked up drivers, bet on the race, and win or lose, put the car back on the lot when they got home. Lee Petty won a 1948 race in a Buick Roadmaster borrowed from a friend. Tim Flock spotted a couple watching practice from their brand new 1949 Olds 88 and talked them into letting him race it. He finished third. In the early days even the most minor changes, such as wedging the springs to provide greater stability in the turns, resulted in disqualification if caught.

But by the late 1940s, modifications for safety, stability, and speed were allowed so long as the cars *looked* "strictly stock." Smart race promoters knew that Chevrolet owners wanted to yell for the cars that looked like theirs, as did Ford owners. Brand loyalty brought customers to the tracks. As Richard Petty recalled in his autobiography *King Richard I*, "With any other form of racing—it didn't matter if it was an Indianapolis car or a hooligan stock car race—the cars weren't anything like you ever saw on the street. This new kind of racing would take street racing to the track. The fans would be watching cars compete that were exactly like the ones they had come to the race in. They'd eat it up."

Today the cars must "look stock" and be "neat appearing." The NASCAR rule book requires cars to weigh not less than 3,500 pounds, including gasoline, oil, and water,

at least 1,600 pounds of which must be distributed on the right-hand side. They must be "steel bodied...American-made passenger car production sedans" of the current and two previous model years, and they must be "NASCAR approved." NASCAR approves each year a limited number of comparably sized Buicks, Chevrolets, Oldsmobiles, Fords, Pontiacs, and other cars. As NASCAR President Bill France Jr. says, "Basically they're close as far as the overall size—as long as their speed is close, that's all we're shooting for."

The engines must be "regular production" engines that are available for "installation and sale to the public in a regular production offering." Most engine parts must "originate from stock production castings and forgings which have been machined according to the normal machining schedule utilized for standard production parts. They may be subsequently refined, modified, and improved by further machining or rework."

But NASCAR rules don't begin to tell you what the cars are really all about and how they're made.

To push 3,500 pounds (which is several hundred pounds heavier than the car in your garage) at a high rate of speed requires substantial horsepower. To do it for four nonstop hours requires reliability and strength undreamed of in production cars. And to keep the big and heavy cars on the oval tracks requires adhesion much greater than, and different from, that of the family sedan. It requires near-perfect aerodynamics, stability, and tires.

The car bodies appear to be stock. NASCAR rules require that "original dimensions of all bodies must remain as manufactured, except for changes which may be necessary for tire clearance." In fact, the bodies are custom made, and very little about them is stock.

Most of the cars are built by Edwin "Banjo" Matthews of Asheville, North Carolina; Hutcherson-Pagan Enterprises in Charlotte, North Carolina; or by Laughlin Racing Products of Greenville, South Carolina. Some of the teams—including Junior Johnson Associates, Hendrick Motorsports, and Richard Childress Racing Enterprises—now build at least some of their cars from scratch. The principal advantages of purchasing a car built by an independent are time and money. Until the advent of multimillion-dollar sponsorships, most teams could not afford to have a crew of chassis builders on their payroll, and the experienced specialists at

Hutcherson-Pagan or one of the other car builders can turn out a car in a week. Teams that are now building their own cars from scratch find that it may take them more than 300 man-hours to complete a single chassis. They believe, however, that the extra quality control is worth the time and money.

Teams work in antiseptic-clean laboratory/garages. The air is filtered continually to eliminate the odors of solvents and grease. Floors are painted to offer a contrast to the metallic-colored engine parts. The fixed equipment, including Magnaflux machines, precision lathes, dynamometers, grinders, and test gear, costs upwards of $1 million. A team may keep a parts inventory of $150,000 or more. The well-heeled teams have budgets of more than $2 million per year, or $70,000 per race. They have 25 or 30 full-time, paid employees, as well as several volunteer weekend warriors who haven't missed a race in years.

At any given time a team's garage may house six or eight race-ready cars, each almost identical in exterior appearance and painted in the vivid colors of the car's sponsor. Typically, a top team might have two short-track cars, for use at Richmond and Martinsville, Virginia, and Bristol, Tennessee, and two superspeedway cars, for use at Daytona, Florida; Talladega, Alabama; and Charlotte, North Carolina. They also may have road-course cars for use at Watkins Glen, New York, and a pair of intermediate cars for use on tracks like Dover, Delaware; Rockingham and North Wilkesboro, North Carolina; and Atlanta, Georgia. There may be 15 or 20 engines and 100 or more rear-end gears. The short-track engines develop high torque at low rpm to provide high performance—acceleration—coming out of tight turns. Superspeedway engines are engineered to run for four straight hours at 8,000 rpm. Each racetrack requires a transmission with different gear ratios.

Most of the teams start with a basic chassis supplied by Hutcherson-Pagan Enterprises or another specialty shop. It consists of a frame, roll cage, dash, fire wall, floor pan, and fuel-cell cage and costs approximately $12,000. Essentially the same chassis could be used for the Bill Elliott Thunderbird as is used for the Darrell Waltrip Chevrolet or the Ricky Rudd Buick. It is the factory-supplied sheet metal skins that are in fact stock and that distinguish a Thunderbird from a Pontiac. Virtually everything else is crafted to order, by hand.

The frame, with a maximum allowable outside rail width of 60 inches, is made from welded steel not less than 0.120 inches thick. A roll cage made of steel bars with a minimum wall thickness of 0.090 inches is welded to the frame and runs from the engine compartment along the sides to the rear of the driver and above the driver's head. The fireproof fuel cell is surrounded by the roll cage. Diagonal reinforcing bars crisscross behind the driver's head and to his right to provide lateral stability. The driver's seat is welded or fastened with aviation-quality bolts to the frame. The aluminum seat is custom-made by ButlerBuilt Motorsports Equipment to fit the individual driver and may have a panel that wraps around the driver's right side to counteract the heavy g-forces of the superspeedways. The sheet metal skins from the factory are reinforced with small-diameter steel tubing.

Superspeedway cars, which run up to 200 miles per hour at Daytona and Talladega, must be as aerodynamically clean as airplanes. They are built to be as narrow as possible, with tires completely tucked inside the fenders. The window behind the driver as well as the passenger-side windows are in place to help clean the car aerodynamically. On the short tracks speeds are lower, and aerodynamics are not as important as at the superspeedways. Short-track cars have the rear side windows removed, which makes them "dirtier" but lets more air in to cool the driver and facilitates wedge adjustments during the race. The wedge-adjustment bolt is over each tire and is usually reached through the engine compartment in front and the windows in the rear. Short-track cars may have fenders and quarter panels made of heavier 0.22-gauge steel to survive the bumping of short-track competition.

Other changes are made as tracks demand. At some tracks it is best to blow all of the exhaust heat on the left rear tire; on others the exhaust is split and vents on both tires. For road courses with right-hand turns and the pits on the right, the filler necks for gas tanks must be on the right side; at all other tracks, gas is poured into the left rear port. On cars for short and intermediate tracks, the brakes are in constant use and are, therefore, in constant danger of overheating, because there is no straightaway time to cool them down. Ram air is forced directly onto the brakes to cool them. On superspeedway cars brakes are used only a few times during a race—slowing down on pit road, or avoiding an accident—and no special cooling devices are needed.

Just as cars vary from track to track, so too do they vary from driver to driver, from driving style to driving style. Richard Petty prefers to drive a high line around the outside edge of a track, hugging the outside wall; Darrell Waltrip prefers to dig down in the corners and hug the inside wall. Each driving technique places different demands on the suspension system, and appropriate adjustments must be made. Some drivers prefer a front-steer car in which the steering box is located forward of the center line of the front axle. Since the biggest load is on the right front wheel, the steering linkage will actually pull the right front wheel in the proper direction. Other drivers complain that front steer lacks sufficient flex and insist on rear steer with the box behind the axle.

Race cars require heavy-duty parts. Cooling systems are oversized to deal with the intense heat of the engines. Fire-proof, steel-bodied fuel cells with a rubberized honeycomb inside take the place of gas tanks. They hold 22 gallons of Unocal 76 high-octane gasoline, the only gas ever used in NASCAR races. The oil system holds 20 quarts, including special oil coolers and reservoirs, and the cooling system holds 10 quarts. Brakes, specially manufactured by JFZ Engineered Products, are designed to keep the super-hot pads from "welding" to the rotors and the rotors from overheating and cracking.

Temperatures inside the car can be 40 degrees higher than in the stands. During the 1987 Talladega 500 when the outside temperature was 95 degrees, CBS broadcast a live picture of a fresh egg frying on the floorboard of Cale Yarborough's car. Use of a "cool suit," in which a freon-type coolant circulates, requires installation of a special pump and reservoir. Most drivers have no other way to remain cool. They lose 8 to 10 pounds of fluids during a race, and most replenish them during pit stops with a gulped-down cup of Gatorade. Some drivers have tried, with little success, to rig up tubes from water bottles. Richard Petty sucks on a wet towel during a race in an effort to remain cool and retain fluids.

Drivers are strapped into their seats with three-inch lap belts, three-inch shoulder harnesses, and two-inch "antisubmarine" or groin belts. Most drivers tighten belts at every opportunity during a race; the more snugly in place they are held, the less chance of a serious injury during an accident.

On the dashboard the drivers see only oil pressure, fuel pressure, ampere, oil temperature, water temperature, tachometer, and rear-axle temperature gauges—all arrayed so that the proper or normal reading is with the needle pointing straight up. A driver can tell in a glance whether any gauge is in an abnormal position.

All of this rides on tires. "The tire is your only connection to the racetrack," says veteran driver Harry Gant. "Everything you try to make the car do depends on those four little spots where the tires touch."

Junior Johnson, six-time Winston Cup Champion car-owner, agrees. "Tires make the difference between tenth place and first place," he says, "and that's a lot of difference."

For many years the only tires used were Goodyear Eagle Stock Car Specials. Goodyear, long the sole purveyor of tires for Winston Cup races, sells them for $177 each and claims to lose money on each sale. A front-running team will use 28 or 32 tires in each of the 29 races on the Winston Cup Series schedule, so a team's tire bill for one race can be more than $5,000 per car or $150,000 for the

season. Goodyear has developed a special tire compound and air pressure for each of the 15 tracks on the Winston Cup circuit.

As the 1988 season began, Goodyear received its first taste of competition in many years from the Hoosier Tire Company of Lakeville, Indiana, owned by the family of R.L. "Bob" Newton. While most of the top teams remained loyal to Goodyear, Hoosier won converts, and races. Hoosier tires were reputed to last longer on the racetrack. Goodyear, in response, changed its compounds to make a quicker and longer-lasting tire.

Mounted on shiny, 15-inch wheels, racing tires are smooth, with no tread. Since adhesion is determined in substantial part by how much rubber meets the road, tire engineers would prefer to see tires running the whole width of the car. NASCAR, however, limits tire width to 13.2 inches for each tire. On most tracks the tires are required to have an inner liner, a tire within a tire. In a high-speed blow-out, the inner tire stabilizes the car, and the driver can limp to the pits.

On 13 of the tracks used on the Winston Cup tour, the cars make only left turns, so the right side of the car travels slightly further. The right-side tires are required to be slightly harder. It is illegal to use the stickier left-side tires on the right. The right-side tires may be as much as one inch larger in circumference than the left-side tires. The difference in circumference is known as "stagger." There is a desirable stagger for each car and each track. If the stagger is off by even 1/100 inch, the car will not handle the way it is supposed to in the turns.

Tires and tracks are organic and change with temperature, wear, and wind. A car may leave the pits with correct stagger, but as the track and the tires heat up, the tires' circumferences grow slightly, and a different stagger may be necessary. Most teams have a tire technician whose job is to keep track of tires and correctly match them to the desired stagger. Stagger changes are, in fact, chassis adjustments—changes in the distribution of weight and balance among the four tires. Reducing the circumference of one tire has the same effect as turning down the wedge bolt on the opposite tire—it puts more weight on that tire. Such adjustments are unique for each car and for each track. If the dominant characteristic of a track is the long straightaway, as is the case at the 2.66-mile Alabama International Speedway at Talladega, where there are steeply banked

turns that generate as much as three times the force of gravity to push a car down and make it stick to the track, a certain stagger and chassis setup are necessary. At tracks where the straightaways are short and there are longer, flatter turns that do not produce high g-forces, a different setup is used.

Experienced crews and drivers know the requirements of each track and can come close to achieving the correct setup before leaving their home shop. However, because track conditions change with fluctuations in temperature, humidity, wind, track wear, and other factors, a setup that initially was perfect may fall apart. During a pit stop, you often see a crew member lean through a window and turn a ratchet that controls a wedge bolt. This has the effect of increasing or decreasing the weight over that particular wheel, much as changing stagger does. The search for the perfect stagger, weight distribution, and chassis adjustment continues to the last lap of a race.

And all the time, the engines are moving these massive machines around the track. Engines are the most mys-

terious and least-understood part of the race car. Veteran racer and car owner Junior Johnson, who is regarded as one of the most knowledgeable men in racing and has done some of the most advanced engine design in the sport, claims that engines are like cakes.

"You mix in the flour, the milk, the yeast, the sugar, the eggs and water, and put it in the oven," he says. "Sometimes it rises four inches, sometimes eight inches, and sometimes it doesn't rise at all. Because you can't see what's happening inside the cake, you can really only guess at the reasons why." There is much trial and error involved in building a fast and reliable engine.

An ordinary car straight from the factory and using a computerized ignition may develop 250 horsepower. The V-8 race car engine develops more than 600 horsepower, using a single four-barrel carburetor and a simple ignition system. To increase horsepower and reliability, engine builders invest up to $20,000 per engine with hundreds of man-hours in labor. A winning team goes through 20 or more engines in a season.

The technology of building high-horsepower engines has been known for years. According to Randy Dorton, who has built engines for drivers Darrell Waltrip, Geoff Bodine, Tim Richmond, and Benny Parsons, "An engine is simply an elaborate air pump. You mix fuel with the air, and you burn it in the cylinders. The more air/fuel pumped through the engine in a given period of time, the more power produced."

Waddell Wilson, perhaps the foremost engine builder now practicing, builds engines for Geoff Bodine's car at Hendrick Motorsports. He says that his 1975 book, *Racing Engine Preparation*, is as current now as when he wrote it.

Top engine builders like Wilson, or Lou LaRosa of Richard Childress Racing Enterprises, or Robert Yates of Ranier/Havoline Racing, command salaries higher than those paid U.S. Senators. They start with a production engine block for a 358-cubic-inch displacement engine. Their goal is not only to triple the horsepower but to strengthen every part in the engine so it will deliver those horses for an entire 500-mile race. A car can be fast and lead for the first 499 miles, but if a $5 part fails and the car falls out, it doesn't earn much money. You can't win if you don't finish.

The block is of production design but is made out of an alloy with a high nickel content for durability. The block itself is checked thoroughly for cylinder-wall thickness and other specifications; factory-poured blocks tend to have irregularities that would prohibit race-level performance. The block is strengthened with heavy-duty, four-bolt main caps to keep it from blowing apart under the terrific internal pressures of race competition. A high-speed grinder is used to clean the burrs and roughness from inside all ports and oil galleys, otherwise unwanted bits of metal could work loose, impede the flow of oil, and enter the lubrication system with engine-crippling results. All parts within the engine—pistons, connecting rods, camshafts, crankshaft, valve trains, and cylinder heads—are hand-crafted by specialists working with special alloys that can withstand the 2,000-degree temperatures and explosive pressures of a high-rpm engine for sustained periods of time. A factory car may turn 3,000 rpm while accelerating; a Winston Cup racer must be able to run 8,000 rpm all afternoon. Every part must be stronger and more reliable than the parts that come from the factory. Each is checked on a Magnaflux machine for invisible cracks. Skilled mechanics run their hands over every part to detect rough or sharp edges.

The Holley carburetors used by virtually every team are larger than those on most factory cars. They have smaller venturis to increase the velocity of the gases and thus the torque curve. Every internal part of the engine is balanced. Although a tolerance to within 1/10 of 1/1,000 gram might be accepted, pistons are balanced against each other to a tolerance of *zero* in order to reduce vibration and friction. Finishing cylinder heads can consume 300 hours of a skilled craftsman's time. Clearances between moving parts are precisely measured to finer than 1/10,000 inch— 1/50 the thickness of a dollar bill—to avoid disastrous metal-to-metal contact. Once an engine has been completed, it is tested on a dynamometer to check for problems and to determine torque and horsepower ratings. Specific problems of a particular engine can be analyzed and corrected by watching readouts on the "dyno."

Different engines are required for different race conditions. At a short track like Richmond or Martinsville, an engine must run in a range from 4,000 to 8,000 rpm. Because of the constant acceleration out of turns into short straightaways and deceleration back into turns, the engines must develop high torque at the bottom end. On superspeedways such as Daytona or Talladega, engines must run in a narrow range between 7,600 and 8,000 rpm for four hours straight, and acceleration is much less important. The power must come at the high end.

Engines last only one race. They are engineered to have a 500-mile life, with a safety margin of 100 miles. After a race, virtually every moving part is examined for wear patterns. Much can be learned, for example, from burns on the piston heads, and parts are then either completely reworked or thrown away. A block may have a life of two or three races before it is junked.

NASCAR's safety rules place strict limits on what can be run. As one builder says, "NASCAR has been at it for 35 years and has closed all the loopholes." NASCAR's goal of promoting close competition requires that all cars be substantially the same, that the only differences be minor adjustments. Dick Beaty, NASCAR's Winston Cup Director says, "The cars are more equal than ever before. This provides the close competition we have."

While NASCAR leadership works to make all cars more equal, and thus more competitive, there's a large group out there working for just the opposite. Car owners and their teams devote time, expertise, and millions of dollars to destroying their competition by making *their* cars the best. A few owners drive their own cars; others are former drivers who have built large operations from the ground up; and some are successful entrepreneurs drawn to the excitement of stock car racing.

Those with the toughest jobs are the owner/drivers. Best known is Cale Yarborough, who started his own team in 1987. Alan Kulwicki, who won the Rookie of the Year Award in 1986, is another. His performance led to a lucrative sponsorship from Zerex Antifreeze. Less fortunate was J.D. McDuffie Jr., who after driving his own car in 600 NASCAR races over a period of 23 years for a total of $1 million, suffered serious burns at Daytona in February 1988. Over a 10-year period, Jimmy "Smut" Means averaged winnings of but $3,600 a race—not enough to pay the tire bill for any of the leading teams. He got the chance to drive a well-shod car for Hendrick Motorsports in one event in 1987 but was involved in somebody else's crash early in the race. Other owner/drivers include Buddy Arrington, Dave Marcis, and Chet Fillip, whose purses have averaged less than $3,000 per race.

A far more comfortable existence has been experienced by former drivers like Junior Johnson and Richard Childress, whose teams have annual budgets reported to be more than $2 million per year.

Johnson even made the intellectual circles as subject of Tom Wolfe's oft-reprinted 1965 *Esquire* profile, "The Last American Hero." He was a driving legend in the hills of the Blue Ridge Mountains of North Carolina before he ever saw a race car. He was outrunning revenuers. "They never caught me drivin'," Johnson says proudly. When they did catch him, however, it was at his daddy's still. After a short prison sentence (he later received a full Presidential pardon), he had a highly successful racing career from 1953 through 1966, winning the Daytona 500 among victories at all the major tracks. Investing his race winnings in a chicken farm, he has become Holly Farms' second-biggest resource, shipping 160,000 chickens every 11 weeks.

But Johnson's greatest success has been as a team owner and car builder. During the 20 years from 1966 through 1986, Junior Johnson cars won more than $10 million dollars. Superstar Darrell Waltrip accounted for $5.5 million of those winnings from 1981 to 1986, with three Winston Cup titles.

Junior insists on having drivers who not only "run for the front and get all there is out of the car" but who also present an articulate image that complements national sponsors like Budweiser, Mountain Dew, and Kentucky Fried Chicken. As a result he has had long-term relationships with top-ranked drivers. Cale Yarborough, before joining the ranks of owner/drivers himself, drove for Johnson for seven years and won three Winston Cup championships and $3 million in the era before big purses. Neil Bonnett drove three years, winning $1.2 million. Terry Labonte became the Junior Johnson driver in 1987.

Not as well known as Junior Johnson as a driver is Richard Childress, owner of the Childress GM Goodwrench Chevrolet piloted by Dale Earnhardt. As an independent driver from 1962 to 1981, Childress's best finish was a third at Nashville in 1978. His total purses as a Winston Cup driver for 10 years were $810,193. In less than a decade as an owner, however, the Childress team's winnings are fast approaching the $10-million level that it took Johnson 20 years to reach. In his extensive shop in Welcome, North Carolina, Childress has one of the most modern and complete race car manufacturing facilities in the world. His GM-backed budget is reported to be $50,000 a week. He insists on quality control to the point where his engine builder, Lou LaRosa, is one of the few to make his own cylinders. His entire crew watches tapes of races on Monday mornings in a private screening room, commenting on the performance, striving for improvement. Such attention to detail has produced the most consistent winning team of the late 1980s.

Other teams have grown from the ambitions of men who, successful in other businesses, have invested heavily in the world of Winston Cup racing. Hal Needham, a former Hollywood stuntman who directed the Burt Reynolds "Smoky and the Bandit" films, teamed with Reynolds to form Mach One Racing. It fielded the Skoal Bandit Chevrolet, driven by Harry Gant, that won more than $3 million in its first five years.

Harry Ranier, whose millions came from pipeline construction and coal mining, joined with J.T. Lundy of Calumet Farm, the home of eight Kentucky Derby winners, to form Ranier/Lundy Racing. Cale Yarborough was its driver in the early 1980s. Then, with Havoline as sponsor of its Ford Thunderbirds, Davey Allison—1987 Rookie of the Year and son of all-time great Bobby Allison—took over.

Chelsea Street Pub restaurant-chain magnate Kenny Bernstein owns King Racing, which runs the Quaker State-sponsored Buick for driver Ricky Rudd. Harry Melling, chairman of the board of Melling Tool Company and Melling Automotive Parts, is owner of the Coors/Melling Racing Ford Thunderbird in which Bill Elliott won the Winston Million, a cash bonus for any driver winning three out of the four biggest races in the Winston Cup season.

The most successful of the outsiders to enter the world of racing is J.R. "Rick" Hendrick of Charlotte, North Carolina, owner of more than 30 auto dealerships and a sometime car and boat racer himself. With Hendrick Motorsports, Hendrick has brought together one of the most talented multi-car teams ever assembled. It's under the direction of Jimmy Johnson, whose background is as an accountant, not as a racer. Driver Darrell Waltrip operates the Chevrolet Monte Carlo SS sponsored by Proctor & Gamble's Tide detergent; Ken Schrader, one of the most talented, articulate, and clean-cut of the younger drivers on the circuit, drives a Chevrolet sponsored by Folgers Coffee; and Geoff Bodine drives the Levi Garrett Chevrolet. Additional backing for Hendrick cars comes from Exxon and AC-Delco Spark Plugs.

Engine builder Waddell Wilson, whose engines gave Waltrip the most durable, though not always the fastest, ride in the team's maiden year of 1987, was said to get a salary of $200,000. Waltrip reportedly received $500,000 plus 50 percent of the purses. The Tide team alone was said to spend $100,000 per race, a sum underwritten by Tide and by Hendrick himself. The Bodine and Schrader teams were reportedly less costly than the Waltrip team but still had operating expenses of $50,000 per race. The astronomical costs aside, Hendrick envisions a day within the next decade when winning the Winston Cup will be worth more than double the $2 million or so it is worth in the late 1980s.

Whoever pays their salaries, the people who build NASCAR cars and engines are, by any measure, the best of American automotive engineers and fabricators. Most receive about the same-sized paychecks they would get at a local garage, but they willingly work 60 or 70 hours per week for far more demanding taskmasters. Their work must be error-free. Even a minor mistake could cost not only a race and an expensive car but also a driver's life.

Some work in secrecy. While the Ronda, North Carolina, shop of Junior Johnson Associates is always open

J.R. "Rick" Hendrick, owner of Hendrick Motorsports.

to visitors, the Dawsonville, Georgia, shops of Ernie Elliott, engine builder for Million Dollar Bill Elliott, the fastest man in NASCAR history, are closed even to those members of the Elliott team whose responsibilities do not include engine building. Engine work is at such an advanced, intense level that Hendrick Motorsports' Wilson says quite correctly, "There's not a lot of people who can tell you things."

Factory engineers cooperate with the race teams. Ford Motor Company is reported to spend close to $1 million per year for each of the Winston Cup teams that race Ford Thunderbirds, providing parts and engineering and technical support. General Motors also backs with money its belief that cooperation with the race teams is a good two-way street; what it learns at the race track, it can incorporate into production cars. Advanced engineering technologies being experimented with at Detroit can be tested on the Chevys and Fords at Darlington. Since the early 1960s, Champion Spark Plug has had its expert available at every Winston Cup event to work with teams to improve spark plug technology. Before 1988 the expert was named Earl Parker; after, Earl Parker Jr.

The bottom line for all this money is winning, yet there is remarkably little cheating. However innovative or efficient, all hardware must meet NASCAR's approval. Before every race, NASCAR inspectors make a visual inspection of the car and the engine, and if anything raises their suspicions, the parts in question are pulled from the engine and calibrated. After every race, the engines of the pole winner and five other randomly selected cars are torn down by NASCAR inspectors. Violations are punished by steep fines or, in the case of oversized engines, by a 12-week suspension. Few teams take a chance. Of 2,184 cars checked in 1986, only one illegal engine was found.

The difference between the winner and the runner-up in a 500-mile race taking three or four hours to run may be less than one second. In the 1988 Daytona 500, Bobby Allison beat his son Davey by a single car length, less than 1/100 second, and won $202,940 to Davey's $113,760.

Race teams spend hundreds of thousands of dollars to look for ways to make their cars hundredths of a mile per hour faster. Many teams spend $1,200 per hour to test in a wind tunnel at the Lockheed-Georgia Company facility in northwest Atlanta. The tunnel contains a 39-foot fan, driven by a 9,000-horsepower engine, which generates winds of 200 miles per hour. Crews monitor delicate in-

struments to determine how minute changes in the profile of the car will improve the way the car slices through the air. The adjustment of the spoiler on the trunk-deck lid can be tested to strike the right balance between "bite," which holds the rear end of the car down on the track, and aerodynamic slickness. Too much bite slows the car; too little bite may increase speed but result in loss of control. In the engine rooms engineers try to improve horsepower and fuel economy. Friction inside an engine running at 8,000 rpm can rob it of as much as 250 horsepower. Experts are studying how to lessen that friction. An increase of even three or four percent in fuel economy could save one 15-second pit stop in a race. Such minimal time savings turn losers into winners.

Advanced computer programs are not only helping to analyze and design engines and improve aerodynamics, they are also helping race teams make strategic decisions during races. At the 1987 Daytona 500—the World Series of Speed—Geoff Bodine was leading Bill Elliott by a margin of 23 seconds with 10 2.5-mile laps to go. His crew chief Gary Nelson estimated that he would probably run out of gas in the last two or three laps. Nelson also knew that a pit stop, even a lightning-quick gas-and-go, would allow Elliott to pass. He made the decision to let Bodine go as long as possible, hoping the gas would last to the final lap and his driver could coast to victory. Bodine, however, ran out of gas three laps from the end, had to coast in for a gulp of gas, and was passed not only by Elliott but 11 more cars.

Months later these numbers were run through a computer. It demonstrated that since the Bodine car used only half as much gas at 175 miles per hour as it did at 200 miles per hour, Bodine could have slowed to 175 miles per hour with 10 laps to go and would have had enough gas to finish and still beat Elliott by three seconds. With this kind of computer-generated information, a team faced with a similar situation in the future might well make a different decision.

Even with available high technology, races are still run and won at the tracks. Most teams leave their home shops on Tuesday night to drive to the track for the following Sunday's race. The race car, fitted with the proper engine and transmission, is loaded onto the team hauler—a Mayflower Moving Van-sized trailer—with a duplicate, backup car. The hauler carries several spare engines and spare parts, tools, and other equipment. Many of the team haulers contain lounges for the driver and crew that have refrigerators, microwave ovens, and other amenities, and cost upwards of $200,000.

Usually a team only takes one car off the trailer at the track, because for each car taken down, a separate entrance fee has to be paid, even if it doesn't run a single practice lap. In case of a wreck during practice or qualifying, the backup car can be entered.

Most teams use a special qualifying engine to run the one or two laps permitted in pre-race qualifying. It does not need to be durable, only fast. At one time in NASCAR history, engine changes could be made during the race, and a skilled pit crew could change a blown engine in under 10 minutes. Now the block cannot be changed, though repairs and replacements can be made.

During the course of practice and during a race, the pit crews communicate with the driver by means of a two-way radio operated on secret, guarded frequencies. Some drivers have little background as mechanics and can only describe symptoms. Others can frequently prescribe solutions. Most teams have spotters stationed around the track and linked to the pit crew by radios. They not only can warn of oil on the track or a wreck ahead that the driver cannot see, but they can spot puffs of smoke coming from the car before even the driver is aware of trouble.

Race fans spend hours arguing whether the driver makes the car or the car makes the driver. Frequently, the fastest car—the car that won the qualifying sprint and thus starts the race from the pole position at the front of the pack—does *not* win the race. Is that because of driver ineptness? Or some slight diminution of power and handling of the car? The debate will continue as long as there are car builders and car drivers.

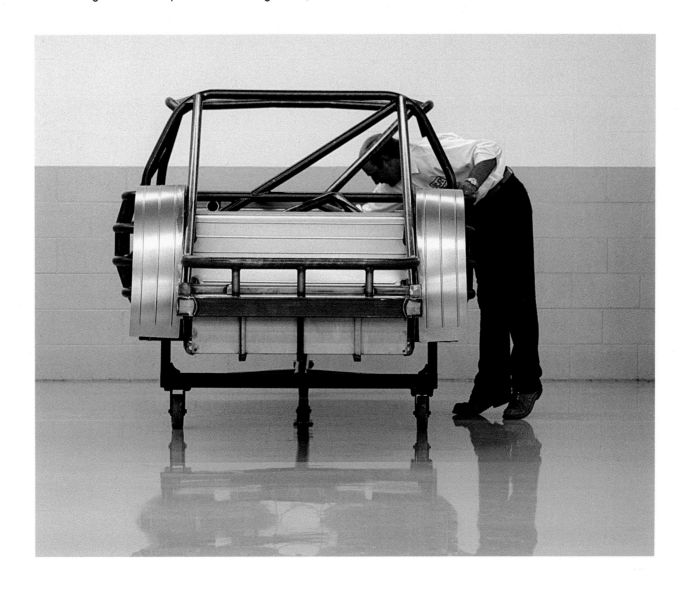

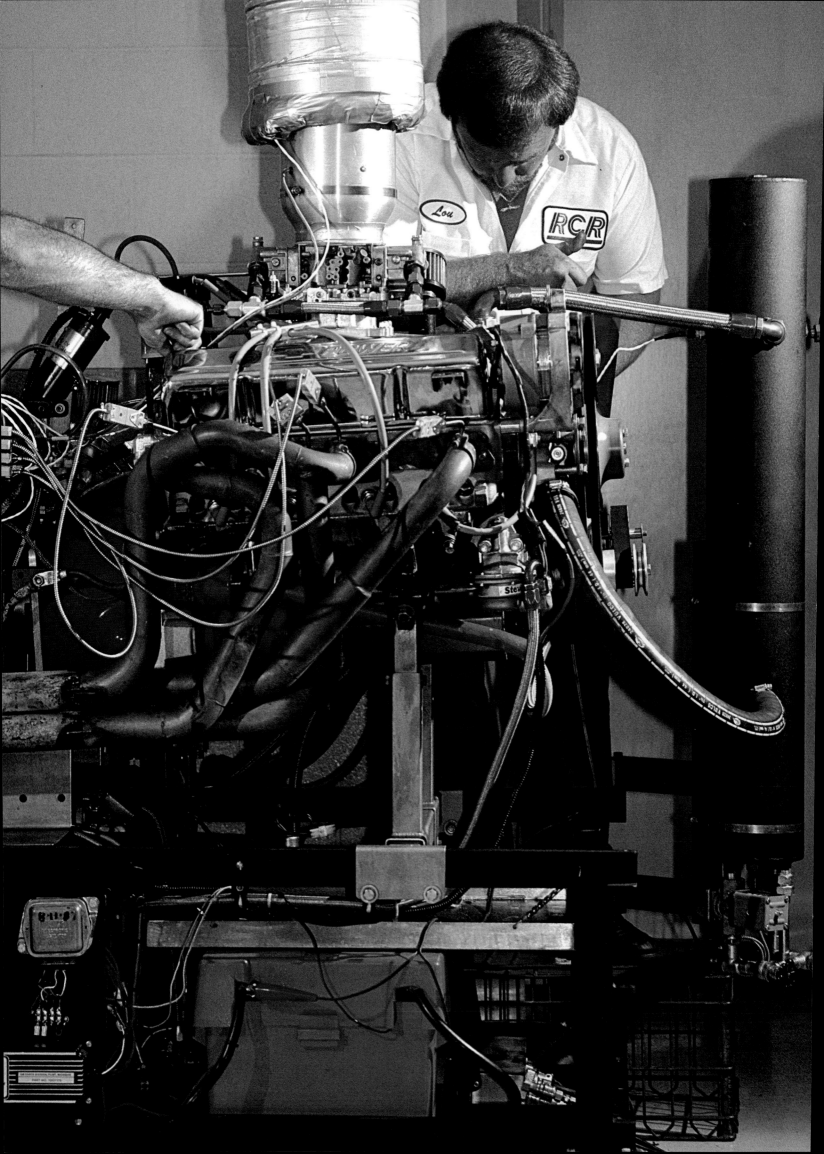

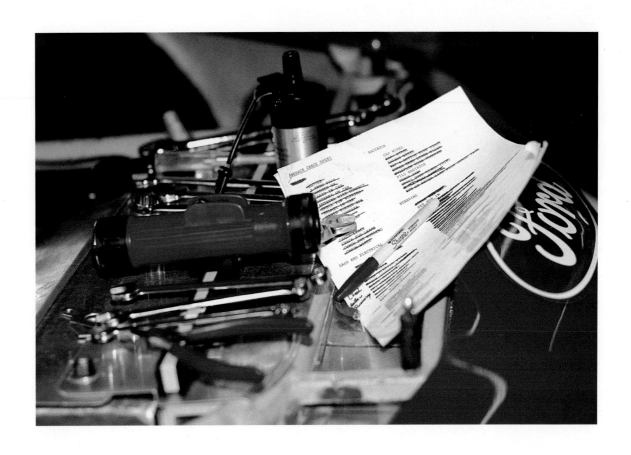

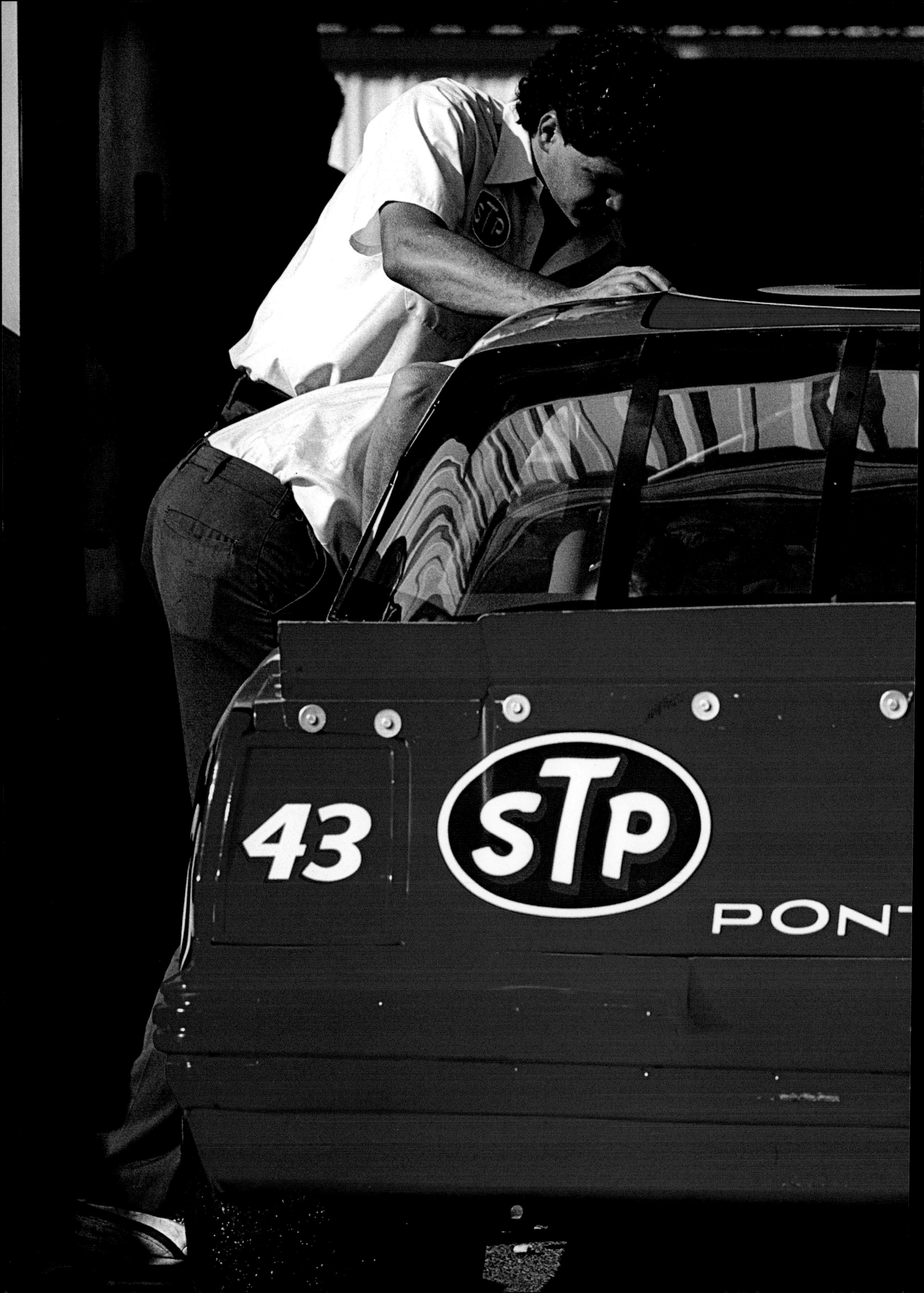
STP
43
STP
PONT

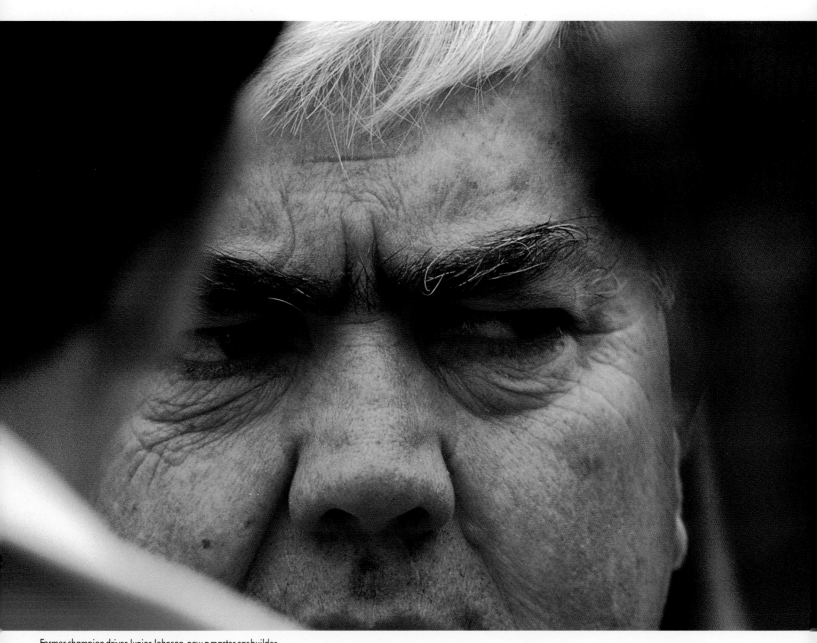

Former champion driver Junior Johnson, now a master car builder,
is the winningest car owner in NASCAR history.

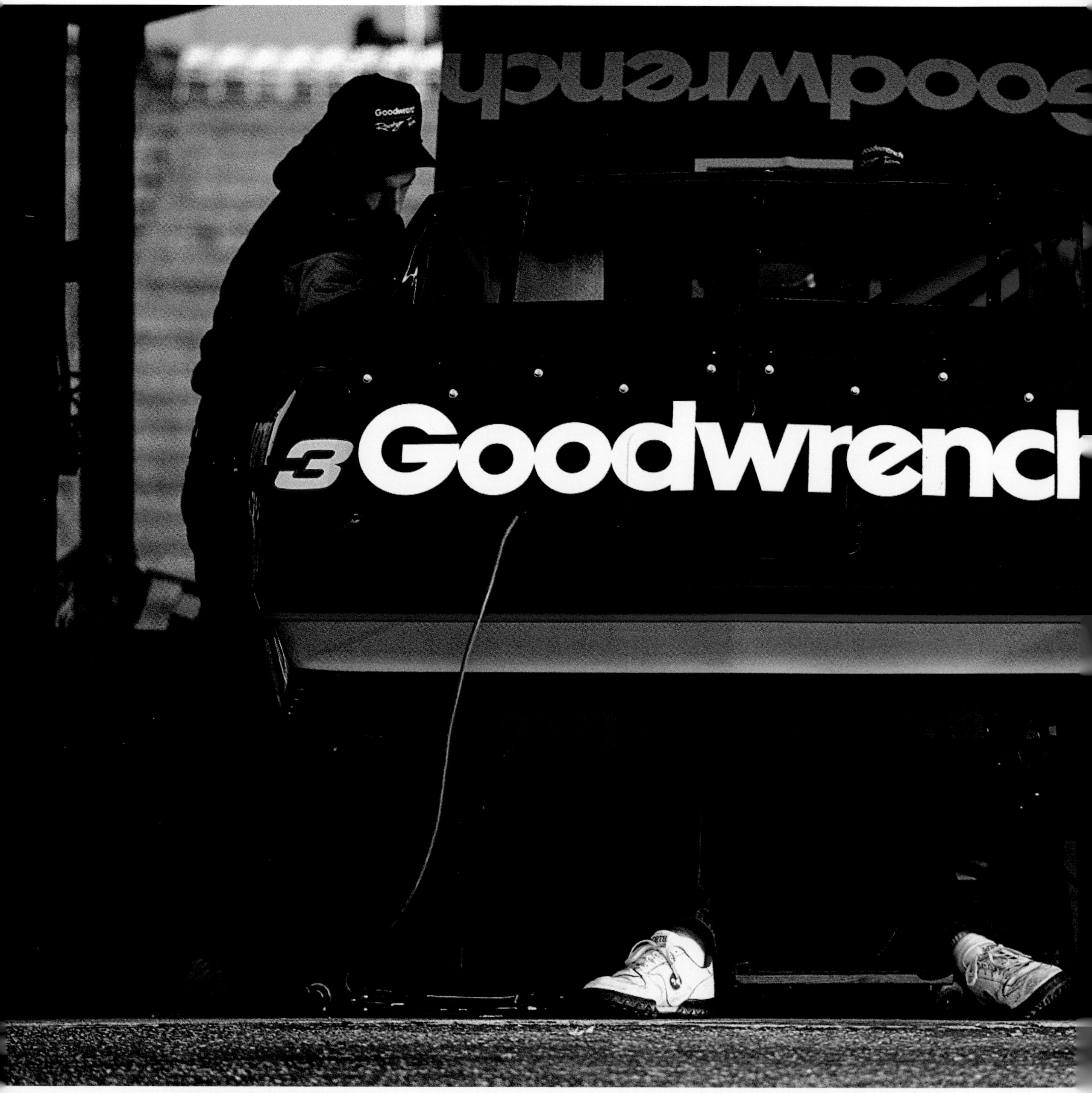
3 Goodwrench
Goodwrench

Dale Inman.

Driver Davey Allison (left) with crew chief Harry Hyde.

Driver Ricky Rudd.

If you saw the 1987 Daytona 500 on CBS-TV, you would have been watching from a camera inside the car of Richard "The King" Petty at the very moment he hit the wall at 195 miles per hour. He was wearing a lap belt, a groin belt, and dual shoulder harnesses, but still he was flung, on national television, from side to side inside the car like a rag doll. Forty-seven years old, The King was racing again the following week.

Later that year at Alabama International Motor Speedway at Talladega, Bobby Allison's Buick actually took off at 205 miles per hour. Airborne, the car skimmed like a frisbee down the front stretch, hit a protective fence, leveled it for a distance of several hundred feet, then turned end-over-end three times. Allison, 50, climbed out of the car and walked away. His son, who had been running just ahead of him and saw it all through his rearview mirror, waved to his famous dad and won the race.

Race drivers have been called speed-crazed lunatics and motorized lemmings. Are they really suicidal maniacs who defy danger? In a psychological study, Keith Johnnsgard of the University of California at Long Beach concluded that drivers are egocentric, self-reliant, and so competitive that they make other professional athletes — including football players — seem like bird watchers. Brock Yates wrote in *The Washington Post* that drivers "are the kind of audacious, defiant, cocky, spit-in-your-eye daredevils you would want on your side in a fight...."

These men — no woman has yet proven a consistent threat — who drive on the Winston Cup level are, first, good athletes. Most were high school football players. All have good upper-body strength and outstanding eye-hand coordination. Many are slight, with darting eyes, and call to mind nimble shortstops or halfbacks. They must have great stamina and powers of concentration in order to drive their 3,500-pound race cars for three or four hours over 130-degree asphalt tracks in the hot summer sun without air conditioning — tightly strapped in, wearing flame-retardant suits and snug-fitting crash helmets with visors.

Age is less of a factor in this sport than in others. Richard Petty in his fifties is as much of a threat to win on any given Sunday as Darrell Waltrip in his forties, Terry Labonte in his thirties, or Bobby Hillin Jr. in his twenties.

One thing you can say for *all* drivers: they are aggressive. Not a single driver is satisfied with finishing second.

Most drivers are tough. Not a single one would back away from a fight or retreat to a corner.

Most of them are loners and have few friends in the sport outside of their teams. They speak cordially in the pits to other drivers, but they do their socializing with their team members, families, and sponsors. You don't want to be too close a buddy to a guy you're going to bang into at 190 miles per hour. They are difficult for outsiders to know well. They believe that they make their living driving cars fast and hard and not by talking with writers. There are a few exceptions, people who are articulate and relaxed in their dealings with the press — Darrell Waltrip, Bobby Hillin Jr., Richard Petty. Waltrip, for example, drove photographer Mark Meyer and me around the track for 30 or 40 laps at Talladega the day before the Winston 500, explaining exactly where he tries to put the car on the track under various conditions.

The good ones are smooth. They do not jerk the car around the track; they let it run around the track. They have superb eye-hand coordination and can hold their rambunctious, fast-moving machines in the groove all the way. They are not afraid to run fast, and that's what they do — in traffic, all afternoon.

To try to get some feel for what driving a Winston Cup car at high speeds is like, I enrolled in the Buck Baker Driving School and took the three-day, basic Winston Cup course, driving around the 1.017-mile oval track at Rockingham, North Carolina. Notwithstanding my love of high speed — I ski on snow and on water and am a licensed pilot checked out in high-performance planes — I couldn't come close to matching Winston Cup speed.

Selecting the profiles for this chapter was difficult. We had to leave out some highly skilled drivers. We tried to include active drivers who have made major contributions to the sport even though they may not be consistent threats to win races today; we included all those who are currently consistent top-10 finishers; and we added a few whose flashes of brilliance indicate that they probably have outstanding careers ahead of them.

Record-setting driver Richard "The King" Petty.

WILLIAM CALEB "CALE" YARBOROUGH

He has been called "the hardest charger who ever lived, the most aggressive race car driver of them all." His record of 3 consecutive Winston Cup Championships (1976-78), 83 victories, and 70 poles will not be topped by many. And though Cale Yarborough since 1980 has been slowly shifting from being a driver to a car owner, he still ranks as a threat to win on any Sunday that he's in the race. He, along with Richard Petty, may be one of the two greatest drivers ever.

Cale Yarborough was born poor on a farm in South Carolina's Pee Dee River delta, but when Spain's King Juan Carlos, a race fan, paid a state visit to the United States in 1976 and had dinner at the White House, he asked to be seated with Yarborough. As a teenager Yarborough worked in a tobacco warehouse for 25 cents an hour. At last report he owned a 3,500-acre farm, 11 Hardee's restaurants, a Goodyear tire store, dry cleaning establishments, a GMC truck dealership, and separate automobile dealerships for Honda (two), Mazda, Buick, and Pontiac. He employs about 1,100 people in the Carolinas and Georgia.

Cale's father died in an airplane crash when Cale was 10. From then on Cale was a tough kid. He once wrestled an alligator, and he was a state Golden Gloves champion.

A good high school running back, he was offered a football scholarship but turned it down. All he wanted to do was race cars. When he was 14, he bought and fixed up a 1930 Ford Model A coupe and raced it down a six-mile straightaway near his hometown on Friday night. Neighbors would say, "There goes Cale!" whenever any loud car roared by. After graduating from high school, he supported himself by playing semi-pro football and running his own logging business, felling trees with an ax and a cross-cut saw. He bought an old Piper Cub, just like his father's, and taught himself to fly in one day.

He loves speed. "That surge of power you feel when the green [flag] comes out is maybe the best feeling in all of racing," he comments. "It rocks you back in your seat as far as you can go, and you feel the blood rush to your shoulders and arms. There's a lightheaded feeling for a second while your eyes catch up with the speed at which the car is suddenly traveling."

Cale came along at a time when he could put this love of speed to good use. "I knew there had to be a better way to make a living than digging around in the dirt and picking tobacco worms off leaves by hand," he said, so he became a race car driver.

Success was neither quick nor easy. During one period when he was 24 with a wife and child, he was sweeping a garage for $1.25 an hour. His first race was the Darlington Southern 500 in 1957. He finished a dismal forty-second and collected a check for $100. He drove his own car on a limited schedule through the mid-1960s, picking up occasional rides with other teams. In the late 1960s, he drove for the Wood Brothers of Stuart, Virginia, winning several hundred thousand dollars in the days before bloated purses. He did not run the full, regular Winston Cup schedule until he joined the Junior Johnson team in 1973. Between then and 1980, he won 55 races, almost 25 percent of all that he entered. That's an extraordinarily high figure. "The King," Richard Petty, has won less than 20 percent of his starts, and the great Darrell Waltrip, who followed Yarborough as Junior Johnson's driver, won 24 percent of his races for Junior but only 16 percent of his career starts.

Cale Yarborough and Junior Johnson remain good friends. When Johnson's regular driver was injured and unable to drive for a time in 1987, Cale was going to drive as a substitute. His sponsor, Hardee's, vetoed the plan because of conflict with one of Junior's sponsors, Kentucky Fried Chicken. Cale, however, released his driver Brett Bodine to drive for Junior.

Cale won the Southern 500 five times—1968, 1973, 1974, 1978, and 1982. "The Granddaddy of Them All," this race is run each Labor Day weekend at Darlington. He visited Victory Lane at the Daytona 500 four times—1968, 1977, 1983, and 1984. In all he has amassed 83 Winston Cup victories.

Unlike some modern racers who work in locked garages protected by security men, Cale has always welcomed visitors to his shop and his home. Of late he has been spending more time with his family. Some years ago, dressed in a conservative suit on his way to a business meeting, he was stopped by his daughter. She reminded him that she had asked him three times to fix her bike. Cale picked up

the phone and rescheduled his meeting, changed clothes, and fixed every bicycle in his garage.

He has curtailed his race schedule. Always one of the more approachable drivers at the race track and always willing to talk, today he is most enthusiastic about his businesses and the number of people he employs. His book written with Bill Neeley, *Cale, The Hazardous Life and Times of the World's Greatest Stock Car Driver* (Times Books, Random House), is as good a stock car racing autobiography as has been published.

Date of Birth: March 27, 1940. **Height:** 5 feet 7 inches. **Weight:** 175 pounds. **Home town:** Timmonsville, South Carolina. **Residence:** Sardis, South Carolina. **Wife:** Betty Jo. **Children:** Julie Anne, Kelley, B.J.

RICHARD LEE "THE KING" PETTY

Richard Petty, the greatest car racer of all time, began his career in 1958 when he entered nine races and earned a total of $960. Since then he has set records that will probably never be broken:

- More than 1,000 Winston Cup races started.
- At least 200 Winston Cup victories (number 200 came on July 4, 1984, at the Firecracker 400 at Daytona, with President Ronald Reagan looking on from the press box).
- First driver to earn $1 million, first to reach $2 million, and so on all the way to $6 million.

His 1967 season, when he won 27 races and had 10 consecutive victories, will be remembered as the greatest race season any driver has ever had. Son of Lee Petty, who won 54 Grand National races (predecessor of the Winston Cup), and the father of Kyle Petty, who won his first Winston Cup victory in 1986, Richard Petty has done it all.

He's tall and skinny as a bean pole. He wears an out-sized cowboy hat, emblazoned with a feather, and wrap-around, dark glasses. If you look in the corner of the lens of his glasses, you'll see the logo of his sponsor since 1972, STP. He has a lifetime contract. He may be the politest and best-liked of all the drivers. His lanky frame can be seen hanging around the garage-area fence long after other drivers have gone home. NASCAR President Bill France says, "Richard Petty, even when he's had a bad day, is the last guy to leave because he's been signing autographs. This has been going on for 25 years, so you have to give him credit."

Petty started racing, as so many did, on dirt tracks in the Carolinas when he was 21 years old and dating a beautiful cheerleader, now his wife Lynda. He had been helping out at Petty Enterprises, working for his father. Against his mother's wishes, he drove a convertible at the Columbia Speedway, a half-mile dirt track in South Carolina, and finished sixth, five laps down. He would have finished higher but for the fact that a car in front of him crashed into the wooden fence and knocked a board into the air. It landed on Richard's head. He kept on driving but lost several positions while counting stars.

Being Lee's son was not necessarily an advantage in the competitive Petty family. Richard remembers his first race against his father, also in 1958. "Cotton Owens was leading the race, and Daddy was running second," he says. "As they came up on me, I moved over to let them pass. Cotton went on by. But Daddy came up and drop-kicked me into the wall." Richard watched from the pits as Lee won the race.

In 1959 Richard thought he had won his first race until a protest was lodged—by Lee Petty. After a check of the score cards, it was determined that Richard was in fact second. You know who was first. Despite that finish, Richard was voted Rookie of the Year.

Richard has not made *his* son's entry into racing any easier than Lee made it for Richard. Kyle drove for Petty Enterprises in a second car from 1979 through 1984. Richard left Petty Enterprises in 1984 to drive for Mike Curb, leaving his son in charge of the family business. At the end of the season, Kyle left in a huff to drive for the Wood Brothers of Stuart, Virginia. Richard realized then what had happened. "We told him we were going to let him run the team," he says. "Then we came in and looked over his shoulder so much he couldn't run it. He said he couldn't live with this, and I don't blame him."

The King has not been above running illegal engines and, what's worse, getting caught. In 1983 at Charlotte, North Carolina, he had an oversized engine, which took him so far out in front that he attracted the attention of NASCAR officials. They took down his engine after the race, stripped him of his victory points, and fined him a record $35,000. Petty claimed he hadn't known that his crew had put in the big motor. "If I'd known, I wouldn't have won the race," Petty says. "I'd have run a close second."

He's had some of the hardest hits in the sport. In a qualifying race at Daytona in 1961 he soared over a guard rail and out of the track. That same day in another qualifying race, his father Lee went over the same rail and was nearly killed. The wreck all but ended Lee's career.

In 1987 at Daytona on national television with an in-car camera that happened to be broadcasting at the time of the crash, Richard hit the wall at 195 miles per hour. "The belts were tight," he remembers. "I couldn't hardly get them loose because they were so tight. The crash took me all the way across the race car. My shoulder hit the roll bar and knocked it out of joint."

His 1988 crash at Daytona has become a feature of every highlight show. First Richard ran into a wreck and spun into the concrete barrier wall. His car rolled over *seven* times. It stopped, and then another car plowed into him.

Since 1978 Richard has been involved in another dangerous game, local politics. Elected as a Republican to the Randolph County Commission in that year, he won 67 percent of the vote in his most recent reelection. He has been mentioned as a candidate for Governor of North Carolina. He may not be the most conservative person in North Carolina, but, "Well, let's just say, I think Jesse Helms is a liberal," he remarks.

Petty has not won a race in several years. In 1987 his son Kyle finished seventh, one slot ahead of him in the Winston Cup point standings. While Richard won $468,602 that year, he also passed his fiftieth birthday. It's a time when many people's reflexes and drive to win lose the edge. His spectacular crash at Daytona the next year certainly gave him an excuse to retire, but The King did not choose to abdicate. "You hate to quit as a loser," he says, "and you aren't going to quit when you're winning. It's about all I know. It's all I want to do. I could do other things, but I'm not interested in them. My whole life has been built around racing. And I hope the rest of it is built around racing."

Date of Birth: July 2, 1937. **Height:** 6 feet 2 inches. **Weight:** 175 pounds. **Home town:** Level Cross, North Carolina. **Residence:** Level Cross, North Carolina. **Wife:** Lynda. **Children:** Kyle, Sharon, Lisa, Rebecca. **Elective Office:** Member, Randleman (N.C.) County Commission (population 100,000).

ELZIE WYLIE "BUDDY" BAKER JR.

"I've never been a 30 percenter at anything," says Buddy Baker. "I like going wide open all the time." He's big; he's rough and tough; and he comes by it all honestly. His Daddy, Buck Baker, who was once a bootlegger, then one of the earliest NASCAR drivers in the late 1940s, and is now in the Motorsports Hall of Fame, says, "For a long time, I felt it was easier to knock them out of the way than it was to race with them. That's the way I drove." Buddy, the tallest driver on the Winston Cup Circuit and a competitor since 1959, may be the best driver never to win the Winston Cup Championship.

He had the reputation of being tough on his equipment. Between 1971 and 1985 he ran 318 races and did not complete 122 of them. Another driver, Tiny Lund, said, "You could give him an anvil in the morning, and he'd tear it up by noon." But also during that period, Buddy won at Talladega four times, Charlotte three times, and at Daytona twice. He drives like he owns the big tracks. Of his 19 Winston Cup Circuit victories, 17 have come on superspeedways. He was the first driver in history to break the 200-mile-per-hour barrier in stock car racing on a closed course, hitting 200.447 miles per hour in a Dodge Daytona on March 24, 1970, at Talladega. He won the fastest Daytona 500 in history—177.602 miles per hour in an Oldsmobile on February 17, 1980.

Buddy Baker has not always been happy racing. "There have been seasons that I really didn't enjoy," Baker says. "I mean, I was winning, but I wasn't having what you would call a good time in racing because of the inner pressure." He wanted to own his own car. "When you drive your own car, frankly, if you get into a little nudging deal on the track, well you do what you feel is best. You don't have to go in on Monday morning and make excuses—'That guy roughed me up, so we got together a little bit.'"

In 1985 he formed his own team with Danny Schiff, president of Bull Frog Knits, a Gastonia, North Carolina, manufacturer of children's clothes. Schiff, a New Yorker, saw a race in 1981 and got hooked. "I've never met one person I didn't like in this sport," Schiff says. He particularly likes Baker. "His reputation is impeccable. I'm in business with somebody you don't have to worry about what he's doing with your money, your people, and your reputation."

Baker says, "This thing came along at a time in my career when I was losing my intensity as a driver. Owning my own team is a new challenge, and to have one of the best teams makes me get off my duff and try harder."

The team did not enjoy overnight success. Buddy did not visit Victory Lane during its first three years and managed only 23 top-10 finishes in its first 65 races. Baker says he underestimated the time it would take to be consistent. "I didn't realize that before you start running, the first thing you have to build is consistency, finishing every race. That's 90 percent of the battle in our sport."

Buddy says the sport has changed dramatically since he was winning in the 1970s. "The biggest thing I've seen change is that there are now 15 cars that can win a race instead of four. Ten years ago there weren't but five teams that could win on a given Sunday. Richard Petty was in that class, and I was fortunate enough to be in it also. One of those few would win. Now take a look. There are so many good drivers there. If you have one bad pit stop or lose a lap for any strange reason, you're out of it because there are so many cars running just as good as yours."

Buddy considers his finest hour to have been his 1980 Winston 500 victory at Talladega. Coming out of his last pit stop, he was almost 20 seconds behind leader Dale Earnhardt. "He was so far ahead, I couldn't see him. I told the crew to call out the differentials—14, 12, 8. At four I told them to quit talking; I had him. I caught him on the white-flag lap. In that kind of deal, you're in your own little world. You're almost mechanical; you're part of the car. The only thing I could hear on those last few laps was the crowd yelling."

Around the track, Buddy is reserved and spends a lot of time tinkering on his car with his two sons. "I've been down so low, I could walk under a snake with a top hat on," he says, "and I've been high enough to think I'd never lose another race. It's been a good experience. I don't know of any job I'd trade it for. If I leave as a driver, at least my driving school gives me a way to stay in racing and help somebody else."

Late in the 1988 season, it appeared that Buddy would indeed leave racing as a driver. Injured in an accident, he later had brain surgery and in September announced his retirement.

Date of Birth: January 25, 1941. **Height:** 6 feet 5 inches. **Weight:** 215 pounds. **Home town:** Charlotte, North Carolina. **Residence:** Mooresville, North Carolina. **Wife:** Coleen. **Children:** Bryan, Brandon.

ROBERT ARTHUR "BOBBY" ALLISON

Bobby Allison was seriously injured in the Miller High Life 500 at Pocono International Raceway on June 19, 1988. Whether or not he races again—and fans everywhere hope and pray that he will—he has earned his place in this book.

Bobby Allison came along at the same time as Richard Petty and has toiled in "The King's" shadow. A few years earlier or later, his reputation would better reflect his accomplishments. As it is, Allison is most-often referred to as the Leader of the Alabama Gang, which sounds more provincial than he deserves. He won the Winston Cup in 1983 and has been voted Most Popular Driver seven times. He is the all-time leader in money won at superspeedways, at almost $5 million for more than 50 victories, and is fourth on the all-time money-won list for all races, with more than $7 million. Though he has less than half as many victories as Petty's 200, Allison has in fact won more money during his career than Petty. Most of his victories came on superspeedways, which have bigger purses than short tracks, while only about one-fourth of Petty's wins were on the long tracks.

Allison is hooked on speed. He almost drowned as a youngster when a motorboat engine he was testing blew up a half mile from shore. That's a long swim in 34-degree water. He pilots his own Piper Aerostars, and in addition to the big Sunday races, he regularly flies to dirt-track or short-track races the same weekend. Piper Aircraft Company sponsors Allison's Busch Grand National division car, and he once accepted delivery of an Aerostar on the front straightaway at Daytona.

Far from being one of those "wild and crazy drivers," he is a solid family man, a devout Roman Catholic who never misses Mass and who also attends the non-denominational prayer service on race Sundays. Not a banger who wins by running other cars off the track, he is a relatively careful driver who avoids trouble, drives his line, and wins or finishes in the top five if his equipment lasts. He has completed almost half of his career races in the top five.

Like all drivers, Allison has survived some spectacu-

lar crashes. One caused the rewriting of the rule book. At the 1987 Winston 500 at Talladega, Allison's car became airborne on the front stretch at 210 miles per hour. Though it knifed through a long stretch of cyclone fence, miraculously no spectators were injured, and Allison walked away from the wreckage. However, it made NASCAR officials realize that cars behaved more like airplanes at those speeds. They mandated use of a carburetor restrictor plate at Talladega and at Daytona, reducing speeds by some 15 miles per hour.

In 1986 Allison began driving for the Stavola Brothers/Miller American Buick team, a two-car team that also features young superstar Bobby Hillin Jr. During his career Allison has driven for the leading car owners, getting 10 wins with Junior Johnson, 14 more with Bud Moore in the early 1980s, then 16 with DiGard Racing.

Allison is one of the better-liked racers. He is a genuine and good friend. When his protégé Neil Bonnett, also a member of the Alabama Gang, was so seriously injured in late 1987 that he planned to give up racing, Allison visited him in the hospital and restored his self-confidence. Bonnett returned to the race track. "I'm really proud of Neil," says Allison, "and if I served as an emotional boost for him, it was only the right thing to do. After all, Neil has been a key friend when I needed one through the years."

Bobby's brother Donnie has been a Winston Cup racer but is no longer active. His son Davey, however, started his Winston Cup career in 1985 and won two superspeedway races in his third season. In the 1988 Daytona 500, won by Bobby, Davey finished second, less than a car length behind.

Allison gives an extraordinary amount of time to charitable causes. He has served as Alabama Chairman for the Muscular Dystrophy Association, the Leukemia Society, and the March of Dimes.

Date of Birth: December 3, 1937. **Height:** 5 feet 11 inches. **Weight:** 160 pounds. **Hometown:** Miami, Florida. **Residence:** Hueytown, Alabama. **Wife:** Judy. **Children:** Davey, Bonnie, Clifford, Carrie.

BENNY PARSONS

When they're not driving, many drivers pass the hours up under their race cars, making minute adjustments—but not big, jolly Benny Parsons. You can find him in the press room, playing cards and telling stories. He's one of the more consistent winners over the years, with $566,484 in 1987 at age 45 and a total of almost $4 million in a career dating from 1964. He is also the best storyteller, working as color commentator for ESPN when he is not driving himself. He may be the best-liked driver on the track. When he won the 1975 Daytona 500, everyone stood and applauded, even in the press box and on pit road. And to top it all, he is humble and self-effacing. When he won the Winston Cup points championship in 1973 with 15 top-5 and 21 top-10 finishes but only one victory, he said, "I just felt like the champion should have won three or four races and been more of a threat at each and every event he went to."

Benny holds a number of important records. He is one of only six drivers ever to have won both the Winston Cup and the Daytona 500. But he is not in awe of himself. Until recently, he'd show up at the track in a "race uniform" purchased off the rack at Penney's, complete with a loop for a hammer!

One of those youths who just didn't know what he wanted to do, Benny dropped out of college and drifted from one automotive job to another. He was pumping gas at his father's garage when two young men he'd never seen before pulled in with a race car on a trailer. They asked Benny if he wanted to go to the race with them; his father said okay, and he's been hooked ever since.

After driving what he could and when he could on smaller tracks, he got his first real racing job at age 23, driving a Ford for the Holman-Moody team in 1964. He struck out badly, finishing twenty-first after starting ninth in his first race. He didn't get a Winston Cup ride again until 1969, when he ran only four races. Finally he became a regular in 1970, driving 45 races and earning $52,375, but he didn't make any significant money until 1977, when he earned almost $300,000.

It was typical of Benny Parsons that at the end of his first successful year, he woke up depressed one Christmas morning. He was thinking of how he had so much, others

so little. That led to the famous Benny Parsons Christmas party for underprivileged families that he has given every year since.

In some of those years, he had some bad breaks. Though he had a successful year in 1981 with three victories and $300,000 in purses, he had to leave the Bud Moore team because he was too nice. The sponsor, Wrangler Jeans, wanted One Tough Customer, Dale Earnhardt. In 1982 he was fired by the Ranier team for not winning at Talledega, one of three Ranier drivers fired that year for not winning. He drove only a part-time schedule during the middle 1980s but in 1986 got the chance to drive the Chevrolet Monte Carlo SS of the Hendrick Motorsports/Folgers Coffee team when that team's regular driver, Tim Richmond, was incapacitated.

"How many chances," asked Parsons, "does a 45-year-old man get to show he still has the fire and ability to drive the full season for a front-line team in this sport? It's been a long time since reporters came up to ask me questions!" He took full advantage of the opportunity, earning more than a half-million dollars for the Hendrick team, but he was replaced at the end of the season by the younger Ken Schrader. In 1988 he drove for old-timer Junie Donlavey in the Ford Thunderbird sponsored by Kraft Foods' Bull's-Eye Barbeque Sauce. He was leading Dale Earnhardt by 20 seconds at Talladega with 62 laps to go, a big upset in the making, when his team let him run out of gas and burn out a piston. He finished thirteenth.

"I feel like my dog died," he said.

But Benny was back the next week, still plugging away and still one of the most respected people in the sport.

In addition to putting on his Christmas party, he has served as president of his local PTA and in other civic activities. He is the owner of Benny Parsons & Associates, which sells auto parts.

Date of Birth: July 12, 1941. **Height:** 6 feet. **Weight:** 200 pounds. **Hometown:** Parsonsville, North Carolina. **Residence:** Ellerbe, North Carolina. **Wife:** Connie. **Children:** Kevin, Keith.

DARRELL WALTRIP

Darrell Waltrip is the racer who led stock car racing into the modern era of mega-corporate sponsorships. Driver of the Chevrolet Monte Carlo SS owned by Hendrick Motorsports of Charlotte, North Carolina, and sponsored by Proctor and Gamble's Tide detergent and by Exxon Corporation's Superflo oils, Waltrip combines movie-star good looks with smooth yet aggressive driving. And it is no coincidence that with the tremendous increase in women fans, he has become a fan favorite. Stevie, his hometown sweetheart, has provided the touch that made Darrell the symbol of today's all-family sport.

In those early years when Darrell, straight out of high school, was learning his trade on short tracks in Kentucky and Tennessee, Stevie was getting her teaching degree at Peabody Institute in Nashville. Pursuing success and so much in love, each shared with the other their outside interests, and together they grew. "Instead of me dragging her down to my level," Darrell says, "she pulled me up to hers."

On his track performance alone, Waltrip has earned his place in the record books. As the 1988 season began, he stood fifth on the all-time win list and had the most wins during the previous 10 years. From the mid-1970s through the mid-1980s, no driver has enjoyed more consistent success.

But his wife's touch sets him apart from the one-time scruffy image of the illiterate redneck driver sponsored by some automotive parts manufacturer. More than any other driver, Waltrip has broadened the audience for stock car racing and enticed the major corporations into spending millions on the sport. Handsome, personable, and articulate, Waltrip not only drives a car for his sponsors but projects his squeaky-clean image and knowledge of their products at off-track appearances. No wonder his car Number 17 is sponsored by Tide and Exxon.

When Waltrip first started his ascent in Winston Cup racing, a driver's skill was the only thing a team owner cared about. Today, that is not enough. To win consistently any driver must have the financial backing of major corporate sponsorship, and to get and keep those sponsors, he must have Waltrip's way with words and clean-cut appearance.

Son of a Pepsi-Cola truck driver in Owensboro, Darrell was a popular student and football player in high school. After graduation he began his education on the race tracks. He made the top circuit when he was 25 and won his first victory three years later. In 1975 he joined Bill Gardner's DiGard Team, had a big win at Richmond, and scored another first off the track when Gatorade became the primary sponsor of the team. Until the Gatorade breakthrough, no product not directly associated with stock cars had been a major sponsor.

By the end of 1980, he had won 27 Winston Cup events and purses of nearly $2 million. He now had confidence to go with his superb, consistent driving skills. When he decided his career would benefit by leaving DiGard, he paid $300,000 to get out of his contract.

Up in the Carolina hills, Junior Johnson was ready for him. With experience gained outrunning revenuers as a bootlegger, Johnson had been a winning driver, then owner of the team for which the great Cale Yarborough drove to three consecutive Winston Cups in the 1970s. One of the most astute men in racing, Johnson could see the coming role of the driver who not only drove like hell but did it with class.

In Junior Johnson's car Waltrip won 43 Winston Cup events, totaling almost $5.5 million in a six-year period. By a wide margin he was the most prodigious winner of his era, winning the championship in 1981, 1982, and 1985 and a race at every major track on the tour at least once. Taking in his share of the winnings and the other plums that fall into a winner's hands, Waltrip's personal earnings in recent years have been in excess of $1 million per year, reportedly making him the highest-paid athlete in the history of the sport.

He moved into an even higher bracket in 1987, joining the Hendrick Motorsports team of Charlotte businessman J.R. "Rick" Hendrick III. The deal is reported to pay Waltrip a salary of $500,000 a year, plus 50 percent of his purses. Hendrick has also given Waltrip the option to buy the team.

What kind of driver can demand this kind of money? Waltrip defies easy analysis as a driver and as a person. He is not a banger, slugging it out on the track, but he will

retaliate when he believes he has been wronged. In 1986 he ran his wrecked car into Dale Earnhardt's. Waltrip — and practically everyone else at the track — thought Earnhardt had intentionally rammed him. Later, however, Waltrip said, "You can't go out there and settle grudges on the race track. Real men settle it behind the garage area."

With his record, he is certainly no wimp on the track either. While his general strategy is to stay on the lead lap and not fall too far behind, he also lies back of the leaders and avoids the banging at the front. Waltrip likes to save his equipment. "You can't win if you don't finish," he says. But in the last few laps, "the fangs really come out."

Typical of the Waltrip style was the final 1986 race at North Wilkesboro, his last race at Junior Johnson's home track. Both wanted to win it for sentimental reasons as well as to add to Waltrip's point total. Waltrip followed leader Geoff Bodine at a safe distance for 50 laps. With 30 laps to go, he started to close in. He tried to pass on Bodine's right, but Bodine slid over, blocking him. Bodine's right rear bumper hit Waltrip's left front. Bodine's bumper was loosened.

Now Waltrip's fangs came out. Like a fighter who has opened a cut over his opponent's eye, Waltrip stalked Bodine. On the short track, hitting 100 miles per hour in the straightaway, 80 miles per hour in the turns, Waltrip began punching Bodine's bumper, deftly tapping it every few yards. If the bumper broke loose, Bodine knew that NASCAR officials would give him the black flag, sending him off the track. Bodine eased off, and when Waltrip started to pass, he had no choice but to grit his teeth and avoid any blocking maneuver or sudden move that might shake the dangling bumper off. Waltrip cruised on by, fans cheering, to win the race.

Articulate and easy with the press, smooth enough to make the inhabitants of corporate board rooms comfortable, Waltrip has one of the fastest, and sometimes most cutting, mouths in the sport. Sometimes his wisecracks are calculated, for strategic advantage, to psych an opponent. Locked in a tight race for Winston Cup points with Dale Earnhardt, Waltrip declined to say anything about Earnhardt to a print reporter. It wouldn't do any good, he joked, "Dale can't read." When he left Junior Johnson, whom he had repeatedly characterized as being "like a father," for Hendrick Motorsports, he told reporters, "This is like getting off an old nag and onto a thoroughbred." Most could not understand such a gratuitous slap in Johnson's face.

He can take it as well as dish it out, however. He repeated, with a laugh, Junior Johnson's riposte to the "old nag" crack. "He told some friends, 'Well, I don't know about nags and thoroughbreds, but last year I had two jackasses and got rid of one of 'em.'"

Most of the time Darrell Waltrip maintains his corporate image. He gives freely of his time to charities. He leads a prayer group every Tuesday morning at his home. He has made television spots to help in the war against drug abuse. He is widely regarded as the most effective and available spokesperson for his sport.

His devotion and gratitude to the woman who stands beside him are open for the world to see. His long-awaited daughter Jessica Leigh is his special pride. He insists on including her in print ads photographed for Tide.

As long as he chooses to drive, Darrell Waltrip will be up at the front of the pack. His lasting contribution, however, will be his leadership of stock car auto racing into the corporate era.

Date of Birth: February 5, 1947. **Height:** 6 feet 1 inch. **Weight:** 190 pounds. **Hometown:** Owensboro, Kentucky. **Residence:** Franklin, Tennessee. **Wife:** Stephanie ("Stevie"). **Children:** Jessica Leigh.

NEIL BONNETT

Neil Bonnett says his previous job as a pipe fitter was more dangerous than driving a race car at 200 miles per hour. "Racing's dangerous, but I've been in a lot worse situations when I was working on tall buildings or electrical plants," he says. He still carries his hard-earned union card. "When I'm in a race car and I see somebody get into the wall, I figure they'll be all right. These cars are built to protect the driver, and the reality is that you can walk away from a pretty good hit. But when you slip off the eighteenth floor of a building, well, reality isn't very pretty."

After, as he says, "escaping" from high school as a teenager, Bonnett was an apprentice pipe fitter. When he finished with work and classes each day, he would drop into the race car shop of Lee Hurley in Hueytown, a suburb of Birmingham. "At first they let me sweep up," Bonnett says, "and then I got a little closer to the cars. After a while, I was doing some of the major work and developed a real liking for it." Soon, Hurley asked Bonnett to drive one of his cars in a Sportsman race at Birmingham. In his second start he posted a victory. In three years Bonnett had won the Alabama State Racing Championship.

Still supporting his new wife and himself as a pipe fitter and racing only on weekends, Bonnett began to drop by the shops of Bobby Allison, also in Hueytown, where he worked on Allison's cars. Once when Bobby was too busy to drive a race in Dallas, he asked Bonnett to fill in. Bonnett won. "After that," recalls Bonnett, "when Bobby had more races than he had time to run—which was all the time—he'd call me up, and I'd drive his cars for him." Bonnett drove as many as 80 races per year as Allison's protégé and by 1974 had accumulated 170 victories. Allison suggested Neil was ready to go on his own.

Allison helped Bonnett find a sponsor, Armor-All, and gave him garage space. Bonnett built his first car himself from the axles up. He started two races in 1974 and two in 1975 but failed to finish any of them. In his fourth race, at Talladega, Alabama, just 50 miles from his home in Birmingham, Bonnett led twice for 12 laps before a blown engine sidelined him. That gave Bonnett the encouragement he needed to expand his program in 1976, when he had one top-5 and four top-10 finishes. Driving for veteran Harry Hyde in 1977, Bonnett earned his first two Winston Cup victories, at Richmond, Virginia, and at Ontario, California.

From 1979 through 1982 Bonnett drove for the legendary Wood Brothers of Stuart, Virginia, winning nine races and six poles. In 1983 Bonnett entered a one-year agreement to race for Rahmoc. In that single year he won at Atlanta and Charlotte and claimed four pole positions. From 1984 through 1986 he was Darrell Waltrip's teammate on the Junior Johnson team. Though he won two races in 1985 and one in 1986, many observers believed that Waltrip got the best equipment and the best pit crew the Johnson team had, so that Bonnett was not permitted to realize his full potential. When Johnson decided to go back to a one-car operation in 1987, he encouraged Bonnett to return to Rahmoc. At the beginning of the 1987 season, Bonnett signed a three-year contract with Rahmoc Racing.

Bonnett likes high speeds. "I wouldn't mind if we drove these cars 250 miles per hour….I get fidgety waiting at a stop light. My bass boat goes faster than 100 miles per hour, and I'm thinking of putting a second motor on it, too."

The real measure of Neil Bonnett was taken in 1987. On October 11 at the Oakwood Homes 500 at Charlotte Motor Speedway, Bonnett was threading his way from the back to the front of the pack. Ricky Rudd's right front fender was touching Bonnett's rear bumper at 150 miles per hour when Bonnett's right rear tire blew. "It exploded so loud," Rudd said, "it scared the hell out of me. It was like a bomb went off. He hit hard."

Bonnett rode straight into the wall between the third and fourth turns. It took 20 minutes of work with the huge metal cutter known as the "Jaws of Life" to cut him out of the wreckage. With a compound fracture of his leg, Bonnett hurt so bad that he couldn't move. "I was in so much pain, I could hardly stand it," he says. "It had reached the point where I was wondering if I would lose my leg."

Just as Bobby Allison had been there to help give birth to Bonnett the racer, Allison was there to give rebirth to his old friend. "I sat there with tears in my eyes," Bonnett recalled. "I was so depressed. I asked him, 'Bobby, how do you do it? How do you keep doing this year after year after some of the things you've been through?'"

Allison told him to be tough and not to give up. He told Bonnett he had to do all he could to come back and race.

Bonnett went home and had a therapy center set up in his house. Three times each day he worked out. He reflected on his career. "I thought about how my career had gone," he told Steve Waid of *Grand National Illustrated*. "I quickly realized that I probably should have won a lot more races than I had. Look at the record: I had been with some of the best teams in racing. Harry Hyde's, the Wood Brothers, Junior Johnson, Rahmoc. Every one of them had been a winner, and I didn't think my accomplishments with them had been nearly enough.

"So while I was sweating and crying on those damn machines, I was driven to the thought that once I did come back, I would be a different racer. I would apply myself more. I would dedicate myself more. I would race hard on every lap at every track. No longer would I be concerned with scratching up another guy's fender. I wouldn't worry about getting someone else upset. I wouldn't worry about negative press, and I wouldn't worry about injury."

And he meant it. Coming back in early 1988, he finished fourth in the demanding Daytona 500, and the following week, he won the Pontiac Excitement 400 at Richmond. His next race was the Goodyear NASCAR 500K at Calder Park Thunderdome near Melbourne, Australia, an unofficial stop on the circuit. Bonnett won again. Next he won the Goodwrench 500 at Rockingham, North Carolina. Three wins in four starts resulted in a season opener that reminded fans of Earnhardt's spectacular 1987 season.

Date of Birth: July 30, 1946. **Height:** 5 feet 8 inches. **Weight:** 175 pounds. **Home town:** Hueytown, Alabama. **Residence:** Bessemer, Alabama. **Wife:** Susan. **Children:** David, Kristen.

HARRY GANT

Harry Gant was trained as a carpenter and was a successful general contractor building houses in Taylorsville, North Carolina, when he decided to do some racing "just to prove to myself I could do it." He raced "for the fun of it." Unlike many of his fellow competitors, Gant didn't start full-time Winston Cup racing until he was 39 years old, the age at which many drivers retire.

While Gant was 24 when he first raced on a track, he had raced as a teenager. "I had my run-ins with the law," he said. "Lots of times the news of what I'd done got home before I did!" When he finally started legitimate racing, it took him only two years to win the Hickory, North Carolina, track championship. He moved up to the late model sportsman class, winning more than 300 races on tracks in the Southeast. He ran his first Winston Cup race, the National 500, at Charlotte Motor Speedway in 1973, collecting $1,760; he ran one or two races in each of the next several years.

In 1978 at age 38, he quit the construction business to become a full-time race driver. He competed for Winston Cup Rookie of the Year in 1979, losing out to Dale Earnhardt. He drove for Jack Beebe's Race Hill Farm team. He won purses totalling $47,185, and his share was 30 percent, but out of that he had to pay his own expenses! "I used to drive to the races and sleep in my van the night before practice started to save money on a motel," he says.

In 1981 he joined the Mach I racing team of Hollywood producer Hal Needham and actor Burt Reynolds, a ride he has held ever since. As a driver for Mach 1, he started almost 200 races and won more than $3 million. It was the first time he made a comfortable living from racing.

Gant has had a solid, successful, but not spectacular career with the Mach I team. Well-financed and using well-prepared equipment, Gant has nonetheless found himself with an unusually high number of DNFs (Did Not Finish). In more than one-third of his races, he failed to complete the race. Many were engine or other mechanical failures; some were accidents in which Gant found himself running into someone else's trouble. But in more than half of the races he started, and in more than two-thirds of those he completed, he ran in the top 10. With career winnings of more than $3.5 million, Gant has one of the more durable and enviable records on the Winston Cup circuit during the 1980s. He finished third in Winston Cup points in 1981, fourth in 1983, second in 1984. He has a career record of nine victories (six on superspeedways) and more than a dozen pole victories. In 1985 he was the International Race of Champions winner.

Unlike some others who have also run into a buzz saw of bad luck, Gant is not a complainer. "I don't try to think about it unless a reporter asks me," Gant jokes. "I just try to put things like that on the back burner and see what happens later on." After getting knocked out of one race by an accident for which he was blameless, Gant went home to Taylorsville, where he owns a steak house, and washed the restaurant's windows.

Richmond (Virginia) *Times-Dispatch* motorsports reporter Harold Pearson wrote of Gant, "As controversial as mom and apple pie, friendly as a young pup, Harry Gant plays one part: Harry Gant. What you see is what he is, no inner volcanos looking for a place to erupt, no axes to grind, wrongs to right—just cars to run, races to win, and friends to meet and greet."

Gant himself explains, "When I started this full time in 1979, I said I wanted to race for another 20 years. I still intend to do that."

Date of Birth: January 10, 1940. **Height:** 6 feet. **Weight:** 190 pounds. **Home town:** Taylorsville, North Carolina. **Residence:** Taylorsville, North Carolina. **Wife:** Peggy. **Children:** Debbie, Donna.

RALPH DALE EARNHARDT

Dale Earnhardt is "One Tough Customer." He wears a scowl and a mustache and walks with a swagger. Fans affectionately referred to Dale's father, the late race car driver Ralph Earnhardt, as "Ironheart;" some drivers refer to Dale as "Ironhead." In The Winston in 1987, his aggressive driving infuriated driver Bill Elliott, who claimed Earnhardt knocked him out of the $200,000 first place. After the race Elliott, who rarely loses his cool or scratches his car, deliberately drove into Earnhardt's car in the cool-down lap.

Long-time fans say that Dale is still trying to please his father, a champion driver in the 1950s. "He was a tough race car driver, a guy who wouldn't give an inch to anybody," Dale recalled to Randy King of the Roanoke, Virginia, *Times and World News*. "I'd sit on the back of a flatbed truck, watching him go around and around, and every lap he made, I made. When I finally got in a race car, it was like I already knew how to drive."

But Dale never won a championship for his father. Ralph Earnhardt had a fatal heart attack while working on a race car in 1973.

Dale does not consider himself a rough driver, and draws a line between deliberately banging other cars and what he calls "rubbin'." He has a point. He's such a good driver that if he wanted to bang someone into the fence, he could probably tell you what hole in the fence he was going to put that person in. "But rubbin' to get by 'em if they're pinching you down, that's *racin*'," he says.

NASCAR officials have not always been willing to recognize such subtle distinctions, however, and have frequently held Dale in the garage area for "consultation." These consultations have cost him races he otherwise would have won.

The controversy that swirls around Earnhardt and dogs him wherever he goes obscures the fact that he may be the most talented all-around driver on the Winston Cup Circuit. Darrell Waltrip, who's had many an all-out racing confrontation with Earnhardt, shakes his head from side to side as he says, "He has the best car. His crew gets him out first. He has about as much natural ability as anybody. He can drive all day and never touch anybody. He can make up a lap anytime he wants to. He's just trying to live up to the One Tough Customer image."

Earnhardt won his first Winston Cup race at Bristol in 1979. That year he also crashed at Pocono and suffered two broken collar bones and other injuries. He still won Rookie of the Year. Next year he won five races and was the Winston Cup Champion. Then in 1982 and 1983, Earnhardt drove Ford Thunderbirds for owner Bud Moore.

"Bud calmed me down in respect to using my head more and driving with finesse and thinking about the end of the race," Earnhardt says. It's not hard to figure why Moore emphasized the end of the race, because the record indicates that in his compulsion to win Earnhardt pushed his cars to the limit. In his first year with Moore, he did not finish fully 60 percent of the races he started, and in 1983 he DNF'd in 13 of 30 races. Earnhardt blamed it on mechanical problems and his belief that Ford gave less factory technical support than Chevrolet. In 1984 he switched to the Richard Childress racing team and Chevrolets.

The Childress/Earnhardt association has been spectacularly successful, winning back-to-back Winston Cup Championships in 1986 and 1987 and more than $4 million in four years. The team has won almost 20 percent of the races it has entered, which is the winning percentage that all-time NASCAR champion Richard Petty ran during the late 1960s and 1970s. No longer tearing up his equipment, Dale received the 1986 Stewart-Warner Track-Force Award for completing the greatest number of racing miles during the season—11,161.7 miles. He finished almost a thousand miles ahead of his closest competitor.

With GM's Mr. Goodwrench as sponsor, Earnhardt credits the Richard Childress team's stability and thoroughness for giving him the best car on the track. Kirk Shelmerdine has been the Childress crew chief since 1981, and Lou LaRosa has been engine builder since 1983. Childress says LaRosa builds "bulletproof engines." Unlike most teams that buy race cars from specialty shops and simply refine and tune them, Childress builds his cars from scratch. "People think you buy parts, and put the car together," Earnhardt says. "Richard buys parts, tests them, and then puts the car together. Then he tests the car. He and his team do things I know other teams don't do. That's what's won the championship."

Earnhardt also gets a several-seconds edge out of the pits. The Childress pit crew, which has won several consecutive Unocal 76 National Pit Crew Championships, not only practices its ballet-like movements but also watches and evaluates videotapes of its performance on Mondays after each race. "It's the most solid, organized, hard-working bunch of guys in the sport," Earnhardt says. "They're almost like brothers...and more than once, it was their efforts that got me into Victory Lane."

Earnhardt can share all the credit he wants, but he can't hide his superb physical and strategic driving skills. In a 1986 race at Rockingham, North Carolina, Earnhardt and Tim Richmond were racing side by side, door handle to door handle, around and around, neither yielding an inch. Richmond pushed Earnhardt down low onto the track, then they both ran up high, almost as if welded together, lap after lap. After a dozen laps, Earnhardt's fresher tires enabled him to power away. In the pits after the race was over, Richmond's crew could not find a trace of paint from Earnhardt's car on Richmond's. For more than a dozen laps, Earnhardt had demonstrated his strength and eye-hand coordination, keeping scant inches between his car and Richmond's. In The Winston in 1987, he maintained control, even while driving across the infield grass to avoid a Bodine/Elliott crash, and won the race. He almost won the challenging Riverside, California, road course by driving straight while other drivers were trying to navigate the "esses."

After two failed marriages, he seems to have found happiness with his wife Teresa, who he says has made him "more of a family person." He has custody of his two children from a previous marriage. "We've gone through it all...the planning, the victories, and the losses. She's been very supportive. I don't ever see a check. And if I need to do some tough negotiating, I send Teresa in."

He has joined St. Mark's Lutheran Church in Mooresville, North Carolina, and says, "It's probably the best thing to happen in my life."

But when it comes time to get behind the wheel and go to work, rubbing and bumping and banging, One Tough Customer rides again. Dale always gets a roar of "Boos" mixed in with cheers and rebel yells when he's introduced. The razzing from the fans disappoints him, but he does not let it take away from his composure or interfere with his driving. "That's what this game is about," he says, "being the coolest and the strongest."

Date of Birth: April 29, 1952. **Height:** 6 feet 1 inch. **Weight:** 180 pounds. **Home town:** Kannapolis, North Carolina. **Residence:** Mooresville, North Carolina. **Wife:** Teresa. **Children:** Kelly King, Ralph Dale Jr.

RICKY RUDD

Ricky Rudd has walked in the footprints of some of the best drivers on the Winston Cup Circuit. In 1981 he was the driver for Bill Gardner's DiGard Racing, following on the heels of Darrell Waltrip. In 1982 he was the driver for Richard Childress Racing Enterprises, following Dale Earnhardt. From 1984 through 1987 Rudd drove for Bud Moore, whose cars have won four Winston Cup Championships. And in 1988 Ricky joined the Kenny Bernstein/King Racing/Quaker State Motor Oil/Buick team. Based on this lineage, Ricky Rudd seems destined to become a Winston Cup Champion in his own right.

Rudd grew up around cars—wrecked ones. His father Al owned a successful salvage yard in Chesapeake, Virginia. When other kids were riding bicycles, Ricky was driving cars around the junk yard. "We could drive 'em, but we could only wreck the parts that were already bad," he says. By the time he got his driver's license, he had probably been in more wrecks than most people endure in a lifetime.

Al Rudd not only let his son drive the junk-yard cars, he encouraged Ricky to compete in go-cart races. Ricky once drove in the Enduro class, in which go-carts hit 120 miles per hour on big tracks. He was national champion several times before he was 16. He raced motorcycles and dirt bikes in high school. He wanted to go to Indianapolis, but that's where Al Rudd drew the line. It costs millions to field an Indy car.

Fortunately for stock car racing, Ricky's friend Cliff Champion, who went on to be crew chief for Cale Yarborough, took him to a Winston Cup race. From then on Ricky was hooked. When he was 19, his father purchased a used race car, and Ricky became the first driver in Winston Cup history to run his first race on that major-league level. It was at Rockingham on March 2, 1975, and 19-year-old Ricky finished a respectable eleventh.

In 1977 his family financed a run for Rookie of the Year. Ricky made it to become, at 21, the youngest driver ever to win the honor. Then it appeared his racing career was through. His family just could not keep the team going without a sponsor. In 1978 Rudd Racing competed in only 13 races, with only four top-10 finishes. The next year he talked fellow Virginian Junie Donlavey, a 30-year racing veteran, into giving him a ride. Steadily improving, Ricky earned four top-five finishes, but another driver brought in a sponsor, and Rudd was released. It looked like he was on his way back to the junk yard, when out of the blue, Darrell Waltrip left DiGard Racing. Ricky took his place in 1981. The next two years—1982 and 1983—he drove for the Childress operation. His first Winston Cup victory was driving a Piedmont Airlines-sponsored Chevrolet in the Budweiser 400 at Riverside in 1983. In his two years with Childress, he won two races and had a highly respectable 26 top-10 finishes in 60 starts.

His affiliation with Moore, starting in 1984, was profitable to both parties. Rudd moved steadily higher in the year-end Winston Cup standings, won more than $2 million in purses, and joined the elite group of racers who stand a legitimate chance of winning a race every time they start. He has demonstrated that he can compete on any track, winning on the road course at Riverside, on the oval at Dover, on the short tracks at Richmond and Martinsville, and on the superspeedway at Atlanta. By the end of the 1987 season, however, Rudd believed he had peaked with the Bud Moore operation and accepted the offer to move on to the Bernstein team. He said that Moore had been "almost like a father" to him. "It just looked like we had leveled off and reached sort of a plateau in winning a couple of races a year," Rudd says. "I guess I'd like to win a few more races a year, and I'm making a change to try to do that."

Of the Bernstein team Rudd says, "They've come a long way in about two years, and I think they're ready to start winning races."

His most difficult victory was at Richmond in 1984. The week before at Daytona, he had been in one of the most spectacular and terrible crashes of racing, when he flipped his car end-over-end eight times. Next day his eyes were black and bloody from the g-forces, but he taped them open and went back on the track. He didn't tell anybody that his eyes were still not focusing properly a week later at Richmond. He just went out and won the race.

As far back as elementary school, Ricky was aware of a pretty girl with long blonde hair named Linda Carwile. After years of courting, they were married in 1979. Linda is one of the most attractive women on the Winston Cup tour, slim and elegant as a model. Many racing wives stay away from the pit area during a race, but Linda sits above the pit in a tennis-referee's chair charting the race, keeping track of gas consumption, and running the stop watches. Ricky and Linda fly to races and to sponsor appearances in their own private plane. They are an attractive, young couple, obviously happy together. Linda has many friends at the races and is as much at ease with them as she was with the Governor and First Lady of Virginia during a reception honoring Winston Cup drivers at the Governor's Mansion.

Ricky characterizes himself as an overachiever, an understatement for a man who won the pole at Riverside in 1988 with his legs in a brace, recuperating from an accident. "Experience is hard to beat. I feel like I've gotten enough knowledge now of all the different race tracks, and now all we've got to do is get the cars to work like I want them to work. If we can do that, then I think we should be up front every race." He says he will not be satisfied until he has a year like Earnhardt had in 1987, when Earnhardt completely dominated the circuit. With his history of walking just behind the leaders, he seems destined to have that kind of dominating year.

Date of Birth: September 12, 1956. **Height:** 5 feet 8 inches. **Weight:** 155 pounds. **Home town:** Chesapeake, Virginia. **Residence:** Chesapeake, Virginia. **Wife:** Linda.

STERLING MARLIN

While Clifton B. "Coo Coo" Marlin was one of the legendary hard-chargers of the early era of stock car racing, running 160 Winston Cup races, he never achieved the fame or results of Lee Petty, Richard Petty, Bobby Allison, or some of the other racing fathers of racing sons. But even if Coo Coo's son Sterling was not born with a silver spoon in his mouth, as motorsports writer Benny Phillips observed, "He did arrive on planet Earth with a valve stem from a racing tire as a pacifier, a lug wrench in one hand, and a stopwatch in the other."

Now pilot of the Piedmont Airlines/Hagan Racing Enterprises Oldsmobile Cutlass, Sterling started in racing as a mechanic and later as crew chief for his father. An excellent high school quarterback, he started driving as a teenager and worked his way up. He was three-time Winston Racing Series champion at Nashville International Raceway, home track of Darrell Waltrip, and in 1982 he was voted "most popular" driver in the Grand American Division. He drove occasional Winston Cup races in his father's car beginning in 1976 at the Music City 420 at Nashville, but 1983 was the first year in which he drove the full Winston Cup schedule. That year Sterling captured Rookie of the Year honors, winning purses totaling $143,564.

Notwithstanding his 1983 successes, he was unable to get a regular ride. He gained experience driving part-time for Roger Hamby, Earl Sadler, Dick Bahre, and Jimmy Means, but he was so insecure about his future in racing that he obtained his real estate sales license, which still hangs with Inman Realtors of Nashville and Franklin, Tennessee. He kept calling potential sponsors. "I probably got a list at home of about 200 companies I contacted in 1985, just trying to get something put together," he says. "That's all I've ever wanted to do, drive a race car and be in Winston Cup. I knew if I didn't keep at it, I would be forgotten."

Finally, in 1986 he landed a ride with Hoss Ellington to drive a limited, 10-race season. Driving the Bull's-Eye Barbeque Chevrolet, he passed Cale Yarborough at the 1986 Daytona 500, finished second in the Firecracker 400 at Daytona, and placed a respectable fourth at the Talladega 500, winning $113,070 on the superspeedways. At the end of the season, when Terry Labonte, who had driven the Piedmont Airlines/Hagan Oldsmobile to a Winston Cup Championship in 1984, joined the Junior Johnson team, Marlin was invited to take his place with the Hagan team. Ellington claimed that he was bound by a four-year contract, but Sterling reportedly paid $100,000 to buy out of the agreement. He took over the Piedmont car at the beginning of the 1987 season. "Everything I've done in my life since attending my first race has been devoted toward getting this chance," Sterling said at the time.

His first season with the Piedmont Airlines team was not the success for which Sterling had hoped. He finished eleventh in Winston Cup points, earning purses of $306,412. In a number of individual races, he enjoyed nothing but bad luck. On his way to a strong third-place finish at Dover in September, his car ran out of gas on the last lap, and he sputtered to a fifth-place finish. He was leading a race at Bristol, when in a much discussed "racing incident," Dale Earnhardt ran under Marlin's car and pushed him up into the wall and out of the race. He was the victim of a stuck throttle on Bobby Allison's car at Rockingham and of his own broken axle at Richmond.

Teaming in 1988 with engine builder Jake Elder, who has built engines for Bobby Allison, Darrell Waltrip, Dale Earnhardt, and other Winston Cup winners, Marlin started the season in the top three. Junior Johnson, whose cars have dominated Winston Cup competition during the 1980s, said of Marlin, "He can win big if he gets the proper breaks. I like him."

Sterling is one of the more cerebral drivers. He is soft-spoken and writes a newspaper column during Daytona's February Speed Weeks. But he's not one to back away from a scrap. "At Martinsville a man can really hold you up if he wants to," Sterling has been quoted as saying. "You just have to go ahead and lay the bumper to him and spin him around."

In addition to selling real estate, he raises tobacco and 500 head of cattle on the 700-acre farm he owns with his father Coo Coo in Tennessee.

Date of Birth: June 30, 1957. **Height:** 6 feet. **Weight:** 180 pounds. **Home town:** Columbia, Tennessee. **Residence:** Columbia, Tennessee. **Wife:** Paula. **Children:** Steadman.

BILL ELLIOTT

They call him "Awesome Bill from Dawsonville" or sometimes "Million Dollar Bill," because in 1985 he won the big Winston bonus of $1 million for winning at Daytona, Talladega, and Darlington. His picture has been published hundreds of times with his smiling freckled face under red curly hair sandwiched between two women in Victory Lane. He's the fastest driver in stock car racing. He performs stunts in his aerobatic plane. He has a Cessna Turbo 210 he uses for business. He's tall and skinny, with a Huck Finn grin.

Surely this must be the most glamorous superstar on the circuit, popular as a rock star, friendly as a car salesman.

Guess again. This is Bill Elliott, a man whose happiest moments, except those he spends with his family and close friends, are all by himself, either wrestling his Coors/Melling Ford Thunderbird around the superspeedways where he builds up his awesome speed, or turning a wrench on that car in his garage to make it possible. "I can't leave the wrench laying," he says. "I've just got to pick it up.

"I'll tell you something right quick about me," Bill Elliott says. Going through the motions of an interview at the insistence of his publicity agent, Bill suddenly came alive. He leaned forward, intensity in his eyes. "If I had $1 or $10 million, I would never change. I just work hard. I work for a living. I work seven days a week lots of times, a lot of hours a day, and it's worth every penny I get out of it."

So the money, glamour, and high life of the superstar mean nothing to Bill Elliott. What does turn him on?

"Competition. That's all there is to it. I've worked hard for what I've got. I started at the very bottom, and I always worked hard. I never give up, and I never will give up."

Maybe someday Bill will cash in on his fame and reputation. "To me, material things are irrelevant," he says. Right now he has all he could possibly want—his car, his garage ("I have put most of the money I won back into my racing."), and his home ("It's a good home. It's by itself with trees around it. I can get away."). People call him a loner. That's not necessarily so. He just doesn't need any more people than he's got.

To understand Bill Elliott you've got to start back in his teenage days in Dawsonville, population 307. His father George liked to own and race cars, but as a small businessman, he couldn't afford to do it on a major-league scale. Bill and his older brothers, Ernie and Dan, pitched in to help, but though they put their time, mechanical knowledge, and sweat into the cars they raced, they couldn't afford one good enough to begin with. From his early teens, Bill put in his hours working either on the Elliott cars or on somebody else's for pay. He showed a talent for driving early, and while still in high school, he was driving the dirt tracks in addition to holding down a full-time job. He married Martha when he was 19, just a few months after meeting her at a roller rink. For the first 10 years of their marriage, they lived where they could, first with her parents, then in an unfinished house, then in a basement apartment. And all the time, he was driving whatever the Elliott family could afford to buy secondhand and fix up.

George Elliott became a Ford dealer, and the quality of the cars gradually improved. Finally, when Bill was 21, the Elliott car finished in thirty-third place at Rockingham—a $640 win! Bill improved steadily over the years, and in 1981 Harry Melling of the Melling Tool Company—with the active encouragement of NASCAR officials who recommended the Elliott operation as a clean, well-run shop—decided he liked the Elliott team, bought it, and financed it. Now all those tough years began to pay off. Brother Ernie proved to be one of the great engine builders, and Bill became known as an accomplished chassis man as well as driver. Within two years, they were running all the Winston Cup races. Coors Beer, trying to expand its name recognition in the Southeast, came in as sponsor, and the package was complete.

In 1985 it almost all came together for Elliott. He won the Daytona 500 in February to start the season. He won $943,203 on superspeedways, eclipsing Bobby Allison's 1982 record of $480,640. He won 11 superspeedway races. But he won only one race after Labor Day and blew a

commanding 208-point lead, allowing Darrell Waltrip to win the season's Winston Cup Championship. Elliott was philosophical about the results. "A lot of times cars fell out of races that were better than mine," he said, "and there were many times when I fell out when I had the better car. You have to put all that into the equation."

Today Elliott is the fastest driver in the history of NASCAR. He has set pole records at every superspeedway on the Winston Cup Circuit and entered the record book with the international, 500-mile, closed-course race record of 188.288 miles per hour set May 5, 1985, at Talladega. In 1985 he won purses and prizes totaling a record $2,433,187. He won the Daytona 500, the World Series of stock car racing, twice—in 1985 and 1987. He has never won the season-long Winston Cup Championship, because he has yet to be a consistent winner on short tracks, on which a third of the races are run. His first short-track victory came at the April 1988 Valleydale Meats 500 at Bristol (Tennessee) International Speedway, the fifty-second short-track race he had run on the Winston Cup tour.

In a typical superspeedway race where Elliott has dominated, he qualifies at, or close to, the front. He starts fast, and applying the horsepower from Ernie's engine, he gets out front and stays ahead of trouble. He manages his pit stops wisely and seldom has to thread his way through heavy traffic from the back of the pack up to the front.

On the short tracks, however, there is simply not enough room to outrun the field. As soon as you get ahead of the pack, you start to lap the slower cars and find yourself in the middle of traffic—the same traffic you have just outrun. Elliott may qualify near the front, but he is not comfortable engaging in the short-track defensive blocking and banging that is necessary in order to get and protect a lead. At one short track in 1987, he started on the pole and finished tenth. Practically every driver who passed him cruised by on his left, rather than being bumped up to the high side where passing is more difficult. "Bill acts like he's still driving his Daddy's car," one of those drivers told me. "'Bill, if you mess up that car, I'll pull you out and put one of your brothers in it, you hear!'"

Perhaps it's just because Bill and the Elliotts, with their background of racing cars bought cheap and held together with mechanical skill, are in the habit of trying to preserve what they've got.

Another characteristic of the Elliott team is their obsession with secrecy. Bill does not hire technicians from the North Carolina area, because he's afraid they might give away his secrets to their friends on other teams. Ernie develops his engines in a locked garage, off limits even to those team members who do not work directly with engines. Bill himself works on the chassis. While many leading drivers spend little or no time working on their cars, Elliott happily spends 12 to 14 hours a day in the garage. "That's where I can get away from it all," he says.

Elliott's spectacular 1985 season may have come too early in his career. In one season he went from a consistent, front-of-the-pack finisher to superstar. He was not prepared for the role of champion and spokesman for the sport. Life in Dawsonville had not trained him to cope with the insatiable demands of fans and press. He sulked and withdrew. His 1986 season was not nearly as successful. Though the fans voted him the Most Popular Driver award for the third straight year, he had difficulties with the press. "If I had been in racing long enough to build up to it a gradual step at a time, it wouldn't have been so hard for me to take," he says, "but to have been thrown in there all of a sudden makes a whole different situation. It just took a whole lot of time to learn how to deal with that."

Bill spent late 1986 and early 1987 deciding what to do. To help improve his short-track performance, he brought in an outside expert. To improve his image he began working on his communication skills. He finished the 1987 season second in Winston Cup Championship points, with 8 poles, 6 victories, and 16 top-five finishes. "To me, we've actually had a better year than we had in 1985," Elliott says. "That's because everywhere we've been, we've been competitive. In 1985 we weren't. I feel like I've come a long way as far as my driving and what I want in a race car." Elliott has been and will continue to be a winner. He is now trying to make himself a Winston Cup champion, and few have any doubt that it will not be long before he succeeds.

And then? "I'm going to work as hard as I can for a number of years," he says, "and then I'm going to quit and do something else and enjoy some time off."

Date of Birth: October 8, 1955. **Height:** 6 feet 1 inch. **Weight:** 175 pounds. **Home town:** Cumming, Georgia. **Residence:** Dawsonville, Georgia. **Wife:** Martha. **Children:** Starr.

TERRY LABONTE

To be chosen to drive Junior Johnson's Budweiser Chevrolet Monte Carlo SS is almost like going to driver heaven. "Junior," says Terry Labonte, who joined the Johnson team in 1987, "has the best ride in NASCAR."

Junior Johnson won 50 Winston Cup races as a driver. In 1966 he stopped driving and formed his own team. His drivers have included Bobby Allison, Cale Yarborough, and Darrell Waltrip. During the 10 years from 1976 to 1985, Johnson's cars won six Winston Cup Championships. When Waltrip left the team for his own version of driver heaven, Johnson could have had his pick of drivers. Why Labonte?

"We wanted a driver who was intelligently aggressive," Johnson says, "and Terry Labonte fits that description perfectly. A lot of drivers might look attractive at first glance, but they fail to meet the standards we've set. They can't perform consistently. Terry meets all our standards."

When Junior called, 30-year-old Terry had experienced just about every peak and valley of racing. At the age of 10, he had won a national title racing quarter midgets. Next step up was stock car racing on short tracks in Texas. His father Bob helped him patch up his cars with parts from the junk yard where he worked and picked up some of his expenses. But the day came when the family just couldn't scrape up the money to tow Terry's Camaro from Corpus Christi to Houston for a race. It looked like Terry was through at 20.

But a track owner who recognized the young driver as a crowd pleaser talked NASCAR team-owner Billy Hagan into supporting Labonte. Two years later Hagan brought Terry to his team's headquarters in North Carolina as a mechanic. Months passed, and Terry became so homesick for Texas and driving that he called his father and said he was quitting. Through at 22.

But his father wouldn't hear of it. "You stick it out," he told his son, and sure enough, Hagan's driver Skip Manning left the team. Terry took his place.

Labonte's first race was the Southern 500 at Darlington, the track that's "Too Tough to Tame." Terry shocked the racing world by finishing fourth. Two years later he came back to Darlington and scored his first Winston Cup victory, beating veteran David Pearson by a fender length. He won the Winston Cup Championship in 1984.

Between 1980 and 1986 Labonte was in the top-10 seven consecutive years, was third in Winston Cup points behind Darrell Waltrip and Bobby Allison, and took in purses worth over $3 million. Then Billy Hagan's company, Stratagraph Inc., entered bankruptcy proceedings, and Hagan gave up direction of the team.

"They sold all our good Chevrolets to competitors and decided to build Oldsmobiles," Terry says. "Things just weren't the same. I checked out." Particularly upsetting to Labonte was that Hagan "withheld" Labonte's share of the Winston Cup Championship prize money won in 1984. "All I got for winning the Championship was a trophy," he said. Labonte heard Junior Johnson was looking for a driver to replace Waltrip, telephoned him, and signed a three-year contract.

Labonte is a perfect fit with the demanding—and winning— Junior Johnson. Labonte respects his automobile and does not race beyond the machine's limits. Between 1981 and 1985 he finished 84 percent of the races he started. In one of his early races, the 1982 Talladega 500, he was racing against Winston Cup Champion Darrell Waltrip in the final lap. Labonte feinted low, then went high, taking Waltrip with him, and finished second. One NASCAR official commented, "Labonte proved something that day. You don't put yourself between Waltrip and the wall with the checkered flag in sight unless you've got guts and want to win. He's not afraid of any of them."

Actually Terry is one of the few drivers who admits he's been afraid. Thinking back to Riverside in 1982 when he piled into a wall going all out, he said, "I broke my foot, my leg, several ribs, and my nose. I got cut up pretty bad. That scared me. On the way to the hospital, I thought I was going to die. I just didn't know. I thought, 'Hey man, is this worth it?' But after a week I started feeling a little better and thought, 'Well, this is just one of those things that happens....'"

Whatever he feels, it doesn't show up in his driving. He's gotten nearly half of his total winnings on superspeedways, although the long tracks account for only one-third of the races.

"I like Daytona and Talladega," he says, "I like running fast."

Handsome and articulate, Terry is an able spokesman for Anheuser-Busch, the team's principal sponsor. "I didn't have to send Labonte to college to teach him how to talk," Junior Johnson says.

"To be with Anheuser-Busch is an honor," Labonte says, "and if that means going to the distributorships and meeting the people, then that is what I want to do."

He has a wry sense of humor. "When I first started driving Winston Cup in 1978," he says, "everybody told me that I got here at just the right time. Richard Petty, Cale Yarborough, and all those great ones would be retired in three or four years. Well, I've been here 10 years, and they're still here."

After an accident that rang his bell, he asked his crew, "Who put the stars under my seat? When I hit that wall, they got out and flew all over the cockpit."

Labonte is also a quick learner. Though he finished the season third in Winston Cup Championship points and won almost $900,000 in purses, the new team had only one 1987 victory and one early 1988 win. Junior Johnson urged Labonte to be more aggressive. "I'm not talking about going up and wrecking people," Johnson says, "I just want him to drive the car more aggressively. Even when he's on the track by himself, I'd like to see him be more aggressive with the car. If you're not aggressive with the car all the time, you get relaxed, and you're not aggressive in the race." Labonte promptly went out and scored an impressive victory worth $200,000 cash in The Winston.

"I think you can call what he did impressive," smiled Johnson. "He definitely impressed me in the last 10 days."

Date of Birth: November 16, 1956. **Height:** 5 feet 8 inches. **Weight:** 170 pounds. **Home town:** Corpus Christi, Texas. **Residence:** Thomasville, North Carolina. **Wife:** Kim. **Children:** Justin, Kristy.

GEOFF BODINE

Most drivers say that winning is the only thing; finishing second is nothing. No driver better lives that maxim than Geoff Bodine, driver of the Hendrick Motorsports/ Levi Garrett/Exxon Chevrolet Monte Carlo SS.

At the Daytona 500 in early 1986, Bodine and Dale Earnhardt were locked in a tight battle for the lead. Each knew he was running out of gas. Each had such a commanding lead over the rest of the field that a quick gas stop might have ensured victory and, at worse, would have resulted in a respectable second-place finish. Neither wanted to get off the track while the other was racing. With two laps to go, Earnhardt ran out of gas, and Bodine didn't. Victory and $192,715 went to Bodine.

Later that season at the Southern 500 in Darlington, rain fell intermittently and stopped the race several times. Bodine and fellow Hendrick Motorsports driver Tim Richmond swapped the lead back and forth. A win for Bodine would give him not only one of racing's most prestigious victories but also a $100,000 bonus from R.J. Reynolds Company for winning two of the "big four" races in a single season. With 35 laps to go, Bodine was leading with only enough gas to last 25 laps. Even a lightning-quick "gas-and-go" would cost him 8 or 10 positions, impossible to get back this late in the race. With the rain and darkness coming quickly, however, there was a good chance that NASCAR officials would have to stop the race. If the race was yellow-flagged, Bodine could splash a couple of gallons of gas in his car and lose only one or two places. He gambled and stayed on the track. The rain lifted, the race continued, and Bodine ran out of gas—finishing in eighth place.

Bodine was born to racing. His father Eli owned the Chemung Speedrome in upstate New York. His younger brother Brett, driver of the Bud Moore/Crisco/Ford Thunderbird, is a Winston Cup star of the future. While still in grade school, Geoff raced micro-midgets and graduated to late-model-type cars on his father's track. By 1978 he had won 55 races in 84 starts in the NASCAR modified division and was ready to move into the major leagues. He moved to Richmond and lived in a motor home next to a tobacco factory. "To this day I still can't stand a motor home," he says. He started three Winston Cup races in 1979 and five in 1981. In 1982 he won a regular ride in a Cliff Stewart Pontiac and started 25 races, winning $258,500

and the Rookie of the Year Award. In mid-1983 he was interviewed by Rick Hendrick, who was then putting together his first Winston Cup team. Bodine was not Hendrick's first choice, but Hendrick admired his persistence, and Bodine landed the ride. Harry Hyde, considered by many to be washed up as a crew chief, was also hired by Hendrick as team manager and crew chief for the Bodine car.

In the new team's first full year, 1984, Bodine started 30 races, won 3, and took home $393,924 in purses. He has increased his winnings each year.

Bodine is deeply but not ostentatiously religious, stoic, and introspective. He had perhaps his share of hard luck in 1986, when engine failures knocked him out of 10 races. Instead of saying, "Well, that's racing," like other drivers, Bodine wondered aloud what "the Lord is teaching me.... He is teaching me to be strong, and He's doing a good job of it...." Geoff takes comfort in the fact that "I meet people every day who share the same feelings I do. There are more Christians around than I ever thought there would be."

As for Rick Hendrick, Bodine says, "His support has seen me through the tough times."

Though he has run close to 200 Winston Cup races and won Daytona, has one of the best rides in racing, and is considered a legitimate star, Bodine is not easy to define as a racer. He is not regarded as a rough driver, though he was fined $15,000 (later rescinded) for allegedly running into Dale Earnhardt in the Charlotte Busch Grand National 300 following a violent running of The Winston in 1987 at Charlotte. Nor is he a flamboyant personality like his former teammate Tim Richmond. He has started in the first row over 30 times—20 percent of his starts—which may indicate that he is better at driving fast during qualifying heats than fast in the traffic of a race. He is not known for pushing and bumping his way to the front when he gets far back in the pack. Instead, he is a skilled and competent driver, one who will continue to attract fan and sponsor support.

Bodine lets you know it when he feels he's getting the short end of the stick. He complained bitterly that his car was blowing engines while "another car within our organization won races and did not blow engines." Of his disappointing 1987 season when he was winless and finished

thirteenth in the Winston Cup points chase, Bodine said, "We constantly lost in the pits and that really works on a driver. It was so bad that before a race, Kathy and I would pray there wouldn't be a yellow, because we knew we'd lose when I pitted. That eventually will tear a driver apart." And, "Engine problems have plagued me for the last three or four years."

All his then crew chief Gary Nelson would say is, "A driver who isn't happy isn't going to win races."

In 1988 Hendrick Motorsports assigned Waddell Wilson, a legendary engine builder and crew chief, to the Bodine team, and Geoff cheered up. "It feels so good to walk into that shop now and know that every engine is for me," he says, "and I don't have to share with anyone. I know that every man there is working with me." Breaking a losing streak of 61 races over two years at the Miller High Life 500 in early 1988, Bodine returned to his old gambling form. "Waddell said that the car had made 39 laps with fuel still in the tank, and he thought we could go the last 41 without stopping again," Bodine points out. "That decision was what won the race."

Date of Birth: April 18, 1949. **Height:** 5 feet 7 inches. **Weight:** 154 pounds. **Home town:** Chemung, New York. **Residence:** Julian, North Carolina. **Wife:** Kathy. **Children:** Matthew, Barry.

ALAN KULWICKI

To appreciate Alan Kulwicki's 1986 Winston Cup season, take a look at some of the other racing operations. There's Junior Johnson's spread in the mountain hollow where he was born near Ronda, North Carolina, complete with chicken house, dog run, helicopter pad, and three large, modern buildings where 55 expert technicians work with the finest and latest engineering equipment. There's the Elliott operation in Dawsonville, Georgia, equally well-equipped but as secretive as a CIA training compound. There are a dozen other such shops, too, throughout the Carolinas, with the enormous, ultra-sophisticated, Charlotte-based automotive factory of the Hendrick racing enterprise bigger than many others put together.

And now enter 31-year-old Alan Kulwicki, a college graduate from Wisconsin, experienced only on the smaller, minor-league tracks in the Midwest, in an open, unapologetic effort to win the Champion Spark Plug Rookie of the Year award. What in particular made Kulwicki's ambition daring to the point of being foolhardy was the equipment he had to do it with: limited financial backing from one sponsor, a single Thunderbird, two engines, two employees, and rented space about the size of the storage room for Junior Johnson's 50-odd transmissions. Kulwicki was his own owner, driver, crew chief, and engine builder. The one duty he delegated, proving himself to be not as crazy as some might think, was publicity. A college graduate in today's world of stock car racing, Kulwicki knew where the real importance lay, for the efforts of Tom Roberts, his publicity man, were certainly a factor in landing his first sponsor, Quincy Steak Houses.

More important, Kulwicki's performance was as good as his publicity. In one car with one spare engine, he entered 23 races and completed 93 percent of the laps. Only Dale Earnhardt, the Winston Cup Champion, had a better finishing record.

Alan finished in the top 5 once, in the top 10 four times, and in the top 15 a total of 14 times. His earnings were $94,450. He won Rookie of the Year all right, for an immediate prize of $10,000 and $1,000 more for each race he started in 1987. He also gained a new sponsor, Zerex Antifreeze, and a bigger budget.

The folks back home, including the Governor of Wisconsin, honored him with Alan Kulwicki Day in early 1987. He flew there in the NASCAR jet.

Kulwicki's success, even with one car, comes as no surprise to the few who know him. In a sport where intense determination is the union card carried by every participant, it's Alan Kulwicki's all-out desire that pushes him to the front of the pack. When he set out to make himself a top driver, he drew a carefully conceived blueprint for his career. He has demonstrated on and off the track that he finishes what he starts.

After graduating with a degree in engineering from the University of Wisconsin, he worked as a mechanical engineer and developed a wheel-alignment system that is still in use. He was also taking night courses toward his master's degree. But that wasn't enough. He had racing in his genes. His father Gerald was a successful crew chief and engine builder on the United States Auto Club circuit. Alan's mother died when he was a boy, and he and his father were especially close. They lived near Milwaukee, where he could hear cars on the fairground's race track. With his father's encouragement, he started racing early and was Midwest Rookie of the Year at the age of 18.

Even with a full-time, rewarding job and graduate engineering courses, he continued racing. In 1980 when he was 25, he chucked his engineering career and went into racing full time on the American Speed Association Circuit of Champions. In a Hardee's-sponsored Pontiac in 1983, he won the Milwaukee Mile, beating NASCAR drivers Bobby Allison, Joe Ruttman, Darrell Waltrip, and David Pearson, who'd all come up to teach the minor leaguers a thing or two. That did it. He was NASCAR bound. He got a ride for five races in 1985, the maximum number he could run and still be considered a rookie the following season. Early in 1986, he moved to Concord in the midst of Winston Cup racing activity, rented garage space for his lone Ford Thunderbird, and began the season that put him on the list of NASCAR drivers to keep an eye on.

Still in the building and growing stage with his team, Kulwicki's obligations as a spokesman for his new sponsor, Zerex Antifreeze, take him away from working on his cars—he now has more than one. He still wants to continue with his own team. "You've got to be careful not to get ahead of yourself," he says. "I'm still learning. If I went to work for a team where everybody had big reputations, there would be a lot of pressure to win right away. If I didn't, it would be my fault—even if the cars just weren't running well."

He believes his engineering education gives him an

edge. "It allows me to understand some things that other drivers may just have to guess about," he says. "But it still takes a lot of experience to be good at racing, and I'm behind quite a few drivers in that respect. I believe my engineering background will enable me to derive better conclusions from my experience, and down the road, I'll be a better, smarter driver."

Kulwicki has himself pretty well figured out. "I need to master how to drive fast, then how to drive fast in traffic, and then how to drive fast in traffic for 500 miles."

His track times show that he knows how to drive fast: in his first three years on the Winston Cup Circuit, he started on the front row five times. A second-place finish at Darlington in 1988 shows he has the stamina to drive fast for the whole race. And anybody who saw the 1987 Miller High Life 400 at Richmond knows he can handle the traffic. In that race when Winston Cup Champion Dale Earnhardt tried to pass him, it was Earnhardt who ended up spinning into the infield as Kulwicki roared away without a scratch.

Kulwicki is intense and determined, like a well-programmed computer. He has not yet shown the flair that makes drivers like Richard Petty, Darrell Waltrip, and Dale Earnhardt stand out from the crowd. But his methodical approach, his obvious intelligence, and his all-out desire have brought him a long way. He will become a major force in Winston Cup racing.

Date of Birth: December 14, 1954. **Height:** 5 feet 9 inches. **Weight:** 160 pounds. **Home town:** Greenfield, Wisconsin. **Residence:** Concord, North Carolina.

KYLE PETTY

Grandson of three-time NASCAR national points champion Lee Petty and son of Richard "The King" Petty, the seven-time Winston Cup champion, Kyle Petty was expected to win a Winston Cup race. But the way he did it was a surprise.

On a bitterly cold day at Richmond with a half-dozen laps to go in the Miller High Life 400, superstars Dale Earnhardt and Darrell Waltrip were racing for the lead. Geoff Bodine and Joe Ruttman were holding down third and fourth. Kyle, in his seventh season, driving the Citgo/7-Eleven Ford Thunderbird prepared by the renowned Wood Brothers, was fifth. Suddenly, Earnhardt and Waltrip collided in what Earnhardt described as a "racing accident" and what Waltrip described as a deliberate hit. Bodine and Ruttman got tangled up in the backstretch wreckage. Kyle snaked his way between smoking cars, went down onto the grass, passed the four disabled leaders in a couple of seconds, and captured his first Winston Cup win.

"It's no secret that we wouldn't have won at Richmond if it hadn't been for bad luck on the part of some of the other drivers and some good luck on our part," he said later. "But if we hadn't been competitive, we wouldn't have been that close near the finish, and the win wouldn't have happened."

The senior Pettys have always been there, in the hunt at the end of the race, in order to take advantage of Lady Luck when she smiled. They've gotten there through thorough race preparation. Kyle is no different.

He won the first race he ever entered, the 1979 ARCA 200 at Daytona, and has been on an upward path ever since. He began racing for his family's Petty Enterprises in 1979. He ran a full schedule in 1981 and won over $100,000 but lost the Rookie of the Year title to Ron Bouchard, who has hardly been heard from since. An outstanding high school athlete who was offered a football scholarship to Georgia Tech, Kyle raced a second car behind his father's famous Number 43 through the 1984 season. Then came a bitter breakup. The friction started, as it does in many two-car teams, with Kyle thinking that his father's car got more money and greater effort from the team than his did. "I had a totally different philosophy from the three of them," Kyle said. "If they went one way, I went the opposite. May-be part of it was just rebellion."

With no Winston Cup wins on his resume, Kyle might have had a difficult time finding a ride. His sponsor, however, Southland Corporation's 7-Eleven stores, thought he had a good future both as a racer and as a commercial spokesman and promised to stick with him if he "went to a competitive team and stayed with Ford." He was accepted by the Wood Brothers, who have owned cars driven by Buddy Baker, Neil Bonnett, A.J. Foyt, Cale Yarborough, Dan Gurney, and David Pearson, among others. Their confidence in Kyle was not misplaced. He won close to $300,000 in his premier season, won a short track (Richmond) in his second season, and a superspeedway (Charlotte) in his third season, taking in almost $1 million in the process.

Like other superstar drivers, he has been accused of rough driving. After an incident at Martinsville in 1986, Ricky Rudd was quoted as saying, "There is an idiot out there on the race track, and his name is Kyle Petty. He turned right into me."

"It was just racin'," Kyle replied. "Two cars got together, and one of them wrecked. I never thought much about it." NASCAR did. It fined Rudd for his comments and Petty $2,000 for rough driving.

The leading vote getter for the Atlanta Invitational in 1986, Kyle is also popular with the fans for his singing and songwriting. He has appeared on TV shows like "Hee Haw." Playing guitar and backed by his five-piece band from Nashville, he has been a show opener for star acts. With an album in the works and commanding $5,000 per performance, he's doing all right in the music department. "But," he says, "it will never take away from my racing. I want to race first. But I feel that racing fame and country-music fame are one and the same. I'm in a position to be a part of all of it. I think I can successfully combine racing and music careers, and if we keep going in the direction we're going in now, I think we have a shot at a championship."

Date of Birth: June 2, 1960. **Height:** 6 feet 2 inches. **Weight:** 195 pounds. **Home town:** Randleman, North Carolina. **Residence:** High Point, North Carolina. **Wife:** Pattie. **Children:** Adam Kyler, Austin Kemp, Montgomery Lee.

RUSTY WALLACE

Rusty Wallace, exuberant and friendly, was not an overnight success. "I hit every bull ring in the United States at least four times," he says with some pride. "I was broke, and I raced my brains out. I paid my dues." While paying his dues, Wallace, son of a race driver in the St. Louis, Missouri, area, collected over 200 short-track victories, was the 1979 United States Auto Club stock car Rookie of the Year, and won the 1983 American Speed Association championship.

Although he drove two Winston Cup races for Roger Penske in 1980 and drove his own car in a handful of races in 1981 and 1982, his big break did not come until 1984 when Cliff Stewart, a businessman from High Point, North Carolina, offered him a ride. With a well-prepared car, Wallace won almost $200,000 with two top-5 and four top-10 finishes, while capturing Sears/Champion Rookie of the Year honors.

Wallace's sophomore year saw an increase in his race earnings to $233,670 with six top-10 finishes, but he did not experience the overall growth and development that he and his owner expected, and he left the team. "Cliff just don't like me too much because of what happened," Wallace says, "but I take my hat off to him for giving me the chance. I like the hell out of old Cliff."

In 1986 Wallace hooked up with the Blue Max team of six-time world drag racing champion Raymond Beadle to drive the Blue Max/Kodiak Pontiac Grand Prix SE. The team was an instant success, winning the Valleydale Meats 500 at Bristol and the Goody's 500 at Martinsville on the way to season-long winnings of $557,354. Fans loved his "go for broke" and "give it everything you've got" style of racing. At the end of one race, Wallace said, "I almost passed out in the car. It was so bad, my face was starting to feel like it was stretching. My neck felt like it was going one way, and my face was going the other. I was feeling like a piece of spaghetti there in the car at the end."

Wallace proved he could win on the short tracks that year. In 1987 he mastered the road courses, winning two of the three road-course events on the Winston Cup schedule. During the Budweiser At The Glen race held at Glenside, New York, on August 10, Wallace led 63 of 90 laps, stopped for gas on the next to last lap, and still beat runner-up Terry Labonte by 11.5 seconds. His victory at Riverside, California, was by a full second over veteran Benny Parsons. He won the last event ever staged at the Riverside course in 1988 before it was bulldozed for a housing development. Finishing the season with 9 top-5 and 16 top-10 finishes, Wallace earned $690,652, bringing him cleanly into the Millionaires' Club. Wallace says of his road course driving, "I go crazy on a road course. I throw the car into corners, run over curbs, things like that. I don't drive very conservatively."

For Wallace, who used to prepare his own chassis, the secret of racing is feel. "You've got to develop a good feel for the race car," he says. "My short-track cars were such superb handling cars. They'd go into a corner and just flat stick. There was no drifting or sliding, and there was no drafting. You'd just go in and hook the corner and go right around it with no slippage." He is still learning how to achieve that same control on the superspeedways. "If you don't know how to draft real well, you're going to get your tail blown away. I wasn't real good at that. I wanted to draft way back, and I'm still not the best at it, but I'm getting better." Midway through the 1988 season, he had apparently learned his lessons very well indeed. He was leading the 1988 Winston Cup points championship race.

Date of Birth: August 14, 1956. **Height:** 6 feet. **Weight:** 175 pounds. **Hometown:** Fenton, Missouri. **Residence:** Charlotte, North Carolina. **Wife:** Patti. **Children:** Greg, Katie, Stephen.

RICK WILSON

When car owner Larry McClure was first looking for a driver for the Morgan-McClure/Kodak Film Oldsmobile, he sought one who was "not afraid to put the pedal to the metal on the big tracks." One driver considered was Rick Wilson, who certainly filled the bill as far as his heavy foot was concerned. But McClure finally passed on him because he was too aggressive.

Today, Wilson does not disagree with that decision. "I had been running on pure guts," he recalls. "I didn't have any experience. I would get in trouble a lot. I would either crash or blow motors, and money started getting kind of thin."

Wilson came up through the short tracks, starting at Auburndale (Florida) Speedway racing the bomber class. "They were six cylinders, and they took pretty well after their names. They were bombs! The first race I went to, I won. From that day on, I was bit!" His first Winston Cup ride was in a rented car at the Firecracker 400 on July 4, 1980, at Daytona International Speedway. He ran with the leaders all day until a mechanical failure dropped him to fifteenth place. But he caught the attention of the national media, who voted Wilson the "Coolest Move of the Race" award.

Working at his family's cattle farm and construction company by day, Rick sank all of his earnings into race cars. He won several short-track events around central Florida and even ran a few Winston Cup races, but he was frustrated by his inability to get a major ride. He was almost at the point of chucking racing. Then in 1984 he built a car for a friend, and the friend backed out of the deal. Rick took the car to the ARCA race in Daytona himself and won. Oldsmobile was trying to increase its involvement in Winston Cup racing at the time, and Rick attracted their

attention. Believing that Wilson had gained experience and maturity and that he had gotten over his tendency to wreck race cars, Oldsmobile put Wilson in the driver's seat of the car that had rejected him, the Morgan/McClure Oldsmobile.

Driving for the Eastman Kodak Company, one of the large national sponsors to have entered the sport within the past few years, has its special burdens. Wilson was sent to a public speaking course by Kodak and drilled on responding to reporters' questions. Now, Wilson can handle the public relations chores with ease. "I've made a lot of appearances for them, and I've done a lot of speaking. The way I look at it, my job isn't done until I've signed every autograph and talked to everybody who wants to talk to me." If he were putting together his own race team, Wilson says he'd hire Darrell Waltrip. "He's an all around driver and an all around promoter," Wilson says. "He'll promote your product for you, and he's a good spokesman."

Wilson, who had career earnings of $213,580 as he entered the 1988 season, was raised in comfortable circumstances. Since the death of his father several years ago, he and an older brother have run the family farm and business. They have diversified into mobile home parks and other businesses and employ over 100 people. Even with his business to fall back on, Wilson plans to race for a long, long time. "When I get too old to drive," he says, "I just want to be remembered as a good race car driver who has done something for the sport. I want to hear people say, 'Rick Wilson was a good race car driver.' That will be worth it all, right there."

Date of Birth: January 31, 1953. **Height:** 5 feet 8 inches. **Weight:** 190 pounds. **Home town:** Bartow, Florida. **Residence:** Charlotte, North Carolina. **Wife:** Teresa. **Children:** Travis.

BOBBY HILLIN JR.

The youngest driver to win a Winston Cup super-speedway event, Bobby Hillin Jr. emphasizes the "Junior" when you first meet him. Unlike many of the other top drivers who grew up poor in the rural Southeast, Bobby grew up in comfortable circumstances in the oil town of Midland, Texas. His father is a successful wildcatter, a friend of Vice President George Bush, and one-time owner of Al Unser Sr.'s Indy car. Bobby wants to make certain you know he is not his father.

When Bobby was 9 or 10 years old, a college friend of his father arrived at the Hillin home one day with a sprint car in tow, looking for a racing partner. The Hillins don't do things halfway, thanks to Grandfather Hillin, an oil-field roughneck whose reputation as a hard, enthusiastic worker enabled him to get his own rig and make some big strikes. Within a few years, Bobby Sr. had the Unser car and a shop in Indianapolis to house it. That's where Bobby Jr. spent his summers. It was his turn to get hooked. His father bought him a mini-stocker that he raced and won with on small tracks in Texas. He went to Buck Baker's driving school in North Carolina to learn stock car racing.

In 1982 his grandfather staked Bobby to a Winston Cup car with veteran crew chief and engine builder Harry Hyde. Hyde encouraged him and improved his driving. Bobby drove five races that year, all on superspeedways, and won the grand total of $9,025. He was 17 years old.

Back in Midland for his senior year in high school, Bobby maintained a 3.8 grade-point average while playing offensive guard and linebacker on the football team. With three months to go before graduation, he made arrangements to complete his school work by correspondence and went to Charlotte, North Carolina—the hub of Winston Cup racing—to be on his own as a full-time driver. He drove 12 Winston Cup races that year, 1983. His hard, consistent driving impressed the Stavola Brothers, Mickey and Bill, who had built up their family rock-quarry business and were looking for an outside interest. They had been thinking about going into Indy racing, but they liked Bobby and financed him for one race at Pocono. It was their first race and, Bobby feared, his last, for his financing had run out. But the Stavolas liked both stock car racing and Bobby Hillin so much that the night after the race they decided to go in all the way. In 1984 the team entered 16 Winston Cup

races with their 20-year-old driver. Bobby Allison helped the young driver land Miller Beer as a sponsor. From 1985 on, Bobby Hillin and the Stavola Brothers team ran the full Winston Cup circuit.

And at his seventy-eighth race on July 27, 1986, at Alabama International Speedway at Talladega, all the dreams came true. Bobby Hillin Jr. threaded his way through a maze of late-race wrecks to win his first superspeedway race and a purse of $60,055.

Bobby is a straight arrow who addresses those even a few years his senior as "Sir" or "Ma'am." The other drivers respect his obvious talent as an athlete and describe him as "a polite young man." He is active in a Christian ministry. While he sips an occasional beer provided by his sponsor, he is intolerant of drugs. "If I thought some other driver was using drugs, I'd whip his butt," he says.

To take the place of the college education he did not get, Bobby has a three-pronged plan for self-improvement. He has set up an organized reading program. He reads the weekly news magazines to keep himself abreast of current events. "I need to learn how to talk with reporters," he says. He subscribes to several financial advisory services in order to manage his growing racing earnings (he passed the million-dollar-earnings mark in 1987). Finally, he is trying to improve his driving skills by imitating the winners. Before a race, he prepares by visualizing himself running the race the way Dale Earnhardt does. Driving a strong car, in which he usually qualifies near the front, has enabled him to run with the Elliotts, Waltrips, and Earnhardts—regular leaders—and learn by observation.

"Racin'," the man-to-man battle that can take place at any time between any two cars on any track, is the great thrill for Bobby. "When I'm not in the hunt, I'm not having fun," he says. "As long as I go out and stand on the gas, I've got a secure job. We've got the best crew and owners on the Winston Cup circuit. Now if I can learn to be a hard charger like Earnhardt, a Winston Cup championship is in my hands."

Date of Birth: June 5, 1964. **Height:** 5 feet 11 inches. **Weight:** 175 pounds. **Hometown:** Midland, Texas. **Residence:** Harrisburg, North Carolina. **Wife:** Kim.

Photo by Steve Matchett

KEN SCHRADER

When Ken Schrader arrived at the top, a coveted ride with the Hendrick Motorsports/Folgers Coffee Chevrolet Monte Carlo, he said, "I'm happy to be here. But I have trouble forgetting about the 14 or 15 years I've raced before I got here. A lot of people haven't seen that."

Like many drivers, Ken comes from a racing family. His father Bill was a legend on tracks in the area around St. Louis, Missouri, where he lives. Ken learned how to drive a home-built car at the age of three and has been driving ever since. He has driven midgets, late-model stock cars, sprint cars, dirt cars, and in 1983 he passed the rookie test at Indianapolis. He drove as many as 100 races a year, sometimes several in one night. The long apprenticeship taught him to adapt to changing conditions. "There's a lot of difference when a Winston Cup track gets a little slick and the groove changes, but it's not near as much as, say, being in Granite City, Illinois, driving a midget in one race and a late-model sportsman in the next." Schrader opted for the big, enclosed Winston Cup cars in 1984. "NASCAR was probably where I always wanted to go."

That year he landed a five-race ride with Elmo Langley, which enabled him to preserve his rookie status. In his first, shortened year of driving the big Winston Cup cars, he never finished in the top 10 and won only $16,425. But he got his next ride driving for W.C. "Junie" Donlavey, who has trained Winston Cup stars such as Jody Ridley and Ricky Rudd.

In the Donlavey Ford Thunderbird, Schrader won Rookie of the Year honors in 1985, following in the groove of Richard Petty, Dale Earnhardt, Geoff Bodine, and Sterling Marlin, and joined an elite group whose winnings topped $200,000 in their rookie seasons. Red Baron Pizza joined the team, and Schrader showed steady if not spectacular progress, finishing 4 times in the top 10 in 1986 and 10 times in the top 10 in 1987, winning $375,918.

In 1987 at Daytona, that most important of all races on the 29-event Winston Cup schedule, Schrader got his biggest victory: he beat Bill Elliott in one of the 7-Eleven Twin 125-mile qualifying races, a stunning upset of "Million Dollar Bill." That, said Schrader, "did a lot for the team and me. It made me realize those guys could be beat." Midway through the 1987 season, the articulate and pho-togenic Schrader began to be seen as a future star. The bidding started.

Bud Moore, one of the winningest Winston Cup car owners of all time, with 267 top-five finishes in 657 races and purses of $5,587,290 between 1961 and 1987, called first. Moore, who has owned cars for Dale Earnhardt, Ricky Rudd, Bobby Allison, and other superstars, believed he had made a deal with Schrader. "We had everything set up, and we were supposed to sign him," said Moore. But Rick Hendrick of Hendrick Motorsports, who owns cars driven by Darrell Waltrip and Geoff Bodine, "got to Schrader at Darlington and just outbid us. I guess it's hard to compete with all that Hendrick money."

Schrader seems to thrive on the attention. "When I go to a grade school to speak," he says, "at least some of the students have heard my name. They don't ask me as often, 'Do you know Dale Earnhardt?'"

Driving the Hendrick car is the culmination of his career. "I don't think you can establish a time frame for the progression of your career in this sport because it's not like you have control of it," he observes. "The budget, the right owner, and the right mechanics, and all of that, plus gaining experience, play a part." With the Hendrick ride, he has access to a big budget, an owner dedicated to winning, and some of the best wrenches in the business. At the AC-Delco 500 at Talladega in July 1988, Schrader won an impressive victory, climbing to fourth in the Winston Cup point standings.

His wife Ann, a nurse in the neonatal intensive care unit at Charlotte Memorial Hospital, is her husband's biggest fan. She runs his fan club from the kitchen table of the Oakwood Mobile Home that is parked on their acreage in Concord. Racing, however, is not her consuming passion. "One reason I wanted to work at the hospital," she said, "was that these people are still oblivious to racing. When you can be with a group of people and not talk racing once in a while, it's kind of nice."

Date of Birth: May 29, 1955. **Height:** 5 feet 10 inches. **Weight:** 190 pounds. **Home town:** Fenton, Missouri. **Residence:** Concord, North Carolina. **Wife:** Ann.

DAVEY ALLISON

He has been hailed as the "best prepared rookie since Dale Earnhardt," and friends joke that it's a good thing Davey Allison's wife is an accountant. "If he wins as much as he is expected to win, she'll have a lot to count," they say.

As the son of racing legend Bobby Allison, Davey was always the focus of high expectations. He has done his part to make them come true. He worked extremely hard on small and short tracks, raced in the lower divisions for years, and by the time he arrived at Winston Cup competition, he was ready. In 1986 he drove a Junior Johnson-owned Chevrolet, filling in for the injured Neil Bonnett, and finished seventh in a car Johnson admits "wasn't handling as good as it should have been." That ride impressed owner Harry Ranier, who signed him as his regular driver for the 1987 season in the Ranier/Lundy Racing/Texaco Havoline/Ford Thunderbird. Texaco U.S.A. President James L. Dunlap said, "My confidence in this team and driver cannot be overstated. I think we have the best in the business."

Allison started off the 1987 season by winning the outside pole position at the Daytona 500, the first time a rookie ever started in the front row in the World Series of racing. He followed his impressive Daytona performance with a win at the Winston 500 at Talladega, a race in which he saw his father survive a heart-stopping crash on the twenty-first lap. Later in 1987, he became the first driver to win two Winston Cup events in his rookie season, capturing the Budweiser 500 on the physically challenging one-mile oval at Dover, Delaware. He easily claimed Rookie of the Year honors and accumulated earnings of almost $400,000, running a limited schedule of 22 races. "Not a bad way to begin a Winston Cup career," said father Bobby. "But it really doesn't surprise me that Davey had such an outstanding season. He has been preparing for this almost all his life. He had to work hard to get the opportunity, and he has every reason to be proud of his accomplishments."

Davey is the first to admit and be thankful for the assistance he has received from his father, the 1983 Winston Cup winner. "It's impossible to say just how much my father has meant to me. He's someone to look up to....He's someone to talk to....And there isn't anything about stock car racing that you can't learn from Bobby Allison."

Davey doesn't believe that being a relatively new driver is all handicap; on some tracks not having to un-learn old habits may even be an advantage. Not too long ago at the high speeds on the superspeedways, each car would leave behind a long trail of low wind resistance. In this draft another car could increase its speed and whip by the first car as though propelled by a slingshot. Improved aerodynamics have changed all this by shortening the length of the draft. Davey says that at Daytona and Talladega where speeds can approach 200 miles per hour, "It's a whole new ball game. I would say that maybe 3 out of every 10 drivers understand what is going on in the draft at these two speedways, and the understanding of the wind currents and wind turbulence helps you avoid what may hinder you. At the speeds we are going now, the old-style slingshot doesn't work anymore. To pass a car that is equal, you have to have someone go with you or catch a car that is out of shape."

Davey does well on the superspeedways. As the 1988 season opened, he won poles at the 2.66-mile Talladega track and the 1.5-mile Charlotte Motor Speedway. He took second at Daytona in the season-opening classic, just inches behind the winner—his father. Two months after Bobby Allison's terrible June 1988 accident and injury, Davey won the Champion Spark Plug 400 at the Michigan Speedway and dedicated the victory to his father. Most racing observers believe that a Winston Cup Championship is certain for Davey Allison.

Date of Birth: February 25, 1961. **Height:** 5 feet 10 inches. **Weight:** 145 pounds. **Hometown:** Miami, Florida. **Residence:** Hueytown, Alabama. **Wife:** Deborah Lynn.

BRETT BODINE

He always wanted to be a racer, but he is equipped to do other things. His father Eli operated Chemung Speedrome, a quarter-mile oval track in upstate New York, and Brett started racing as a youngster. In addition to his locally famous father, his brother Geoff, older by 10 years, was active in racing and hired Brett as his crew chief when he was still a teenager. But if he cannot make it as a racer, Brett, who holds an associate degree in mechanical engineering from State University of New York, can work in that field. Or he could be a body fabricator, a trade he pursued in North Carolina while waiting for his big break in stock car racing.

Brett's breaks came quickly. His first race was in 1976 in a 1965 Buick that he drove in a street-division race at Chemung. He raced modifieds while he was in college, beginning in 1979, and moved into the Busch Grand National cars after moving to North Carolina in 1984. He drove for the noted short-track car builder Robert Gee and picked up victories at Martinsville, Bristol, and Rockingham. He got his first full-time ride in 1986 in the Busch Grand National series, being tapped by Howard Thomas to drive the Thomas Brothers Country Hams Oldsmobile. In his maiden season he entered 31 events, got 24 top-10 finishes, and was second in point standings, with winnings of $173,000.

In 1987 Brett combined the best of both of the top-two NASCAR stock car divisions, the Busch Grand National and the Winston Cup series. He continued his driving duties for the Thomas Brothers and enjoyed a second consecutive year earning well in excess of $100,000. He also signed on to drive the Winston Cup cars of Hoss Ellington in 14 races. His biggest break, however, was driving in two races for Junior Johnson, the winningest owner of all time, when Johnson's regular driver, Terry Labonte, was sidelined with a broken shoulder blade. Driving for Johnson, Brett finished eighth at North Wilkesboro and ninth at Bristol.

The successes and experience of 1987 led to a 1988 contract with one of the top teams in the Winston Cup division. Brett was selected by Bud Moore to drive the Ford Motorcraft/Crisco Thunderbird. Moore, who has owned cars driven by Buddy Baker (1975-77), Bobby Allison (1978-80), Dale Earnhardt (1982-83), and Ricky Rudd (1984-87), has won more than $5,587,290 with 58 career wins as an owner.

Brett was elated. "This is going to be a great team," he said. "It's a great opportunity for me to step into a ride of this caliber. It will be my first full-time season. I never expected this to happen so quickly."

And Moore, who has taught so much to so many young drivers, says, "Brett is going to do a good job for us. He has a tremendous amount of racing experience, and he is very familiar with the fundamental working of a race car. I can't think it will take too long to prove we've put together a good combination." Indeed, Brett proved his mettle on the Winston Cup Circuit with a fourth-place finish at the World 600 at Charlotte Motor Speedway in 1988.

Date of Birth: January 11, 1959. **Height:** 5 feet 7 inches. **Weight:** 165 pounds. **Home town:** Chemung, New York. **Residence:** Harrisburg, North Carolina. **Wife:** Diane. **Children:** Heidi.

Three-time Winston Cup champion Dale Earnhardt (left) talks to car owner
Richard Childress before a race.

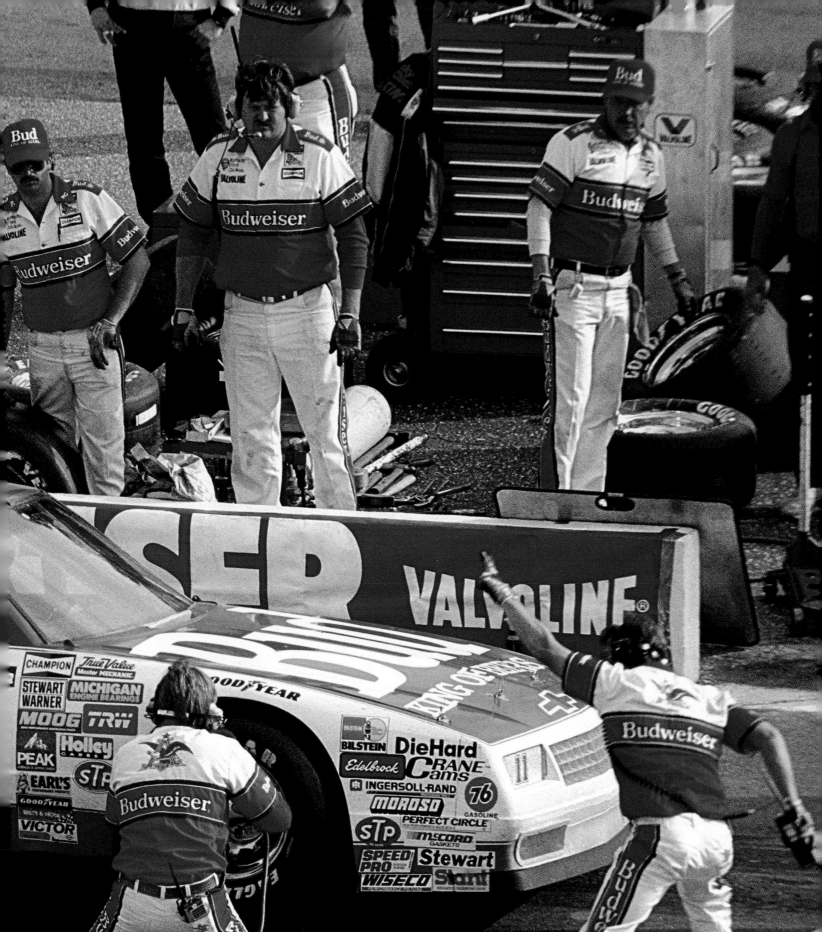

Driver Dale Earnhardt.

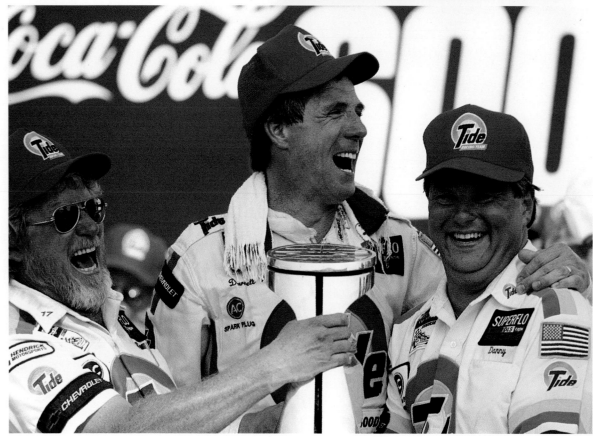

What is NASCAR? Ask a driver, and you'll hear that NASCAR is the organization that hands out fines for rough driving. Ask a car owner, and you'll be told that NASCAR helps locate additional sponsors for cars. Ask a track owner, and you'll learn that NASCAR sanctions the races and hands out the prize money. Ask some fans, and you'll see that even if they know what you are talking about, they probably won't know what the acronym stands for. And if you ask NASCAR's top officials, you'll hear them say, "We're in the entertainment business. The people who buy the tickets and go to the events go to be entertained, to relax, and to enjoy the race. We promote competition, but it is also entertainment."

NASCAR—the National Association for Stock Car Auto Racing— is all of those, and more.

To understand how NASCAR works, start by climbing up to the control tower high over the grandstand some Sunday afternoon. The eagle-eye observations and split-second decisions made in that plain little room can determine the outcome of the race.

The tower room, with peeling paint and straight-backed, metal chairs, is crowded the minute the first man walks into it. He's Les Richter, NASCAR Vice-President for Competition. Not too many years ago as the All-Pro defensive end for the Los Angeles Rams football team, he was throwing quarterbacks around for a living. An hour ago, he was supervising NASCAR's pre-race technical inspection of the cars. Now he's in charge of the race.

Joining him are Ed Cox, Administrative Competition Director; Dick Beaty, Winston Cup Director, who conducted the pre-race meeting of the drivers; and Robert Black, Director of Emergency and Rescue Operations. They can see the entire track beneath them, and they have radio contact with red-jacketed NASCAR officials spotted around the track. They know, too, that someone on each crew is listening in on the NASCAR frequency.

To most people everything looks fine down on the track—but not to Richter. As the crowd sees the brightly colored, roaring cars start around the track on their warm-up laps, Richter spots something else. Little grains of dust.

"Run five laps under caution," he tells the pace car. "Run the middle one fast to get the dust off the track."

The race begins when Richter is satisfied the track is

safe. The men in the crowded tower watch. They comment. Nothing escapes them.

"Shepherd's loose!" Richter suddenly barks. "Watch him." Only after two more laps does it become apparent to the fans that Morgan Shepherd's Number 26 car is sliding out to the right on the turns. Out of 32 cars blasting around the track, Richter has picked out the one car that might cause an accident. The driver's pit is notified, the car called in for adjustments. NASCAR works for safety.

There's a wreck on the track! "Show the yellow," Richter commands the flagman suspended over the raceway. Ed Cox, the cleanup guy, takes over. He is under intense pressure. The fans are restless. They came to see racing, not the caution car leading a bunch of zombies around the track. Ed thinks also of the people he can't see, the ones watching the race on TV a thousand miles away. After 10 laps under caution, the track appears to be clean.

But not to Ed. "Get that piece of sheet metal on turn three," he says. He sees the reflection of a puddle of oil. "Sta-Dri high on turn two." And only then, at last..."OK, let's go racin'!"

This is a short track, with bumping and banging in the corners. It's a rough track, too, and it's hard to hold close to two tons of race car in the groove at 100 miles an hour.

Derricke Cope slides his car into the wall between turns one and two. Even before Richter can get the yellow flag displayed, down on the track Darrell Waltrip, leading the race, slows down. The pack falls in behind him. "Thanks, D.W.," says Beaty into his radio. He knows that Waltrip's pit crew is eavesdropping on the NASCAR frequency and will pass the word along.

Richter's eye grabs onto car Number 8, driven by Bobby Hillin Jr. Back in the pack, away from the action, Hillin is swinging out on the turns for no apparent reason, bumping whoever passes him. "Hillin's loose," Richter says. Once again he has spotted what amounts to a foul away from the ball. He radios to the track. "Tell the Number 8 car that he's not on the lead lap and he's holding up traffic." Far below, a red-jacketed NASCAR official walks to Hillin's pit. The crew chief gets the message and radios it to Hillin.

Bobby is defiant. He slides out again—and this time he loses control! He spins! "Show the yellow!" NASCAR

Les Richter, NASCAR Vice President for Competition.

commands. For the first time the crowd is aware of Hillin; thousands rise to their feet. He regains control and starts back in the race. The brief excitement is over.

But not for Richter. He takes a scorecard, writes on it, and holds it up for the world to see—$250. That's Bobby's fine for "intentionally stopping on the track."

And so it goes until the last of 400 laps, when Neil Bonnett edges Ricky Rudd for the win after a last-lap sprint. It has been a safe, relatively uneventful race with close competition, thanks to the NASCAR men high above the track.

The story of NASCAR begins with William Henry Getty "Big Bill" France, the founder of modern-day stock car racing. France grew up in the Maryland suburbs of Washington, D.C., in the 1920s. He was an enthusiastic stock car racer. Following his marriage to Anne Bledsoe in 1931, he headed south to Florida.

France settled in Daytona Beach and opened a service station on Main Street. A civic booster as well as a racer and fan, he talked the city fathers into putting on an auto race in 1936. He laid out a 3.2-mile race course that ran north on the hard-packed sand of the beach and south on a parallel highway, U.S. Route A1A. The ends were connected by short runs through soft sand. The City of Daytona Beach sponsored a February race on the beachroad course in 1936, and the local Elks Lodge sponsored it in 1937. Both lost money. Enter Big Bill, six foot five, weighing 240 pounds. He promoted the 1938 race himself and, with 5,000 fans each paying a 50-cent admission, cleared a profit of $200. The following year he upped the admission price to $1 and increased his profit margin 11-fold to $2,200. Big Bill was off and running.

By 1947 France was promoting 8 or 10 races per year on the National Championship Stock Car Circuit. He could see a host of problems in the stock car business. Rules changed from race to race. A car that would be legal at one track for one promoter might be illegal at another track where a different promoter wrote his own rules. Worse than that, unscrupulous promoters would literally "fly-by-night" with the gate proceeds. Racers would labor all week as bus drivers or truckers or salesmen, work on their cars at night, race on the weekend, and discover that the promoter had taken off with the purse.

Even when the promoter stayed on to give out the prizes, the money was disappointing. Louis "Red" Vogt, an Atlanta garage owner who built cars driven by France, recalls promises of $2,000 purses. "When we got through with the racing, all of us—the drivers, mechanics, car owners, and whatnot—would split about $400. The winner seldom got his guarantee."

Many in the grandstands were so unruly that men were afraid to bring their wives and children to watch the races. Yet conditions were ripe for the sport. The postwar boom had dramatically increased the number of cars on the road after years of gas rationing and no automobile production. People were interested in cars and in watching them race, and now they had gas and the itch to go. It was time to bring order to the chaos, to establish a sport that would progress and prosper, a national sport with a national championship.

Once again, enter Big Bill France. On December 14, 1947, he convened the First Annual Convention, as he called it, of the National Championship Stock Car Circuit at the Streamline Hotel in Daytona Beach. About 15 promoters,

racers, and garage owners from around the East Coast attended. They selected the name National Association for Stock Car Auto Racing despite some good-natured wrangling from those who felt that the acronym "NASCAR" sounded too much like free advertising for the then popular Nash car. Four of those present accepted the invitation to buy stock in the organization. Its business, formally stated, was to sanction races for a fee. Individual members would pay dues.

It was agreed that races sanctioned by NASCAR would be run according to uniform standards set by the technical committee, appointed by Bill France. The committee formulated "1948 Rules and Regulations" governing engine size ("Any block can be oversize"), safety ("All drivers must be strapped in and must wear safety helmets"), and fair competition ("Foreign manufactured cars will not be permitted").

The first NASCAR-sanctioned race was the Winter 160 at Daytona Beach on February 15, 1948—promoted by Bill France. In its inaugural season NASCAR sanctioned nine races. By 1950 there were 395 NASCAR sanctioned races.

NASCAR suggested safety standards for the tracks it sanctioned, requiring, among other things, safety fences to keep errant wheels from flying into the spectator stands. NASCAR's rules mandating technical standards ensured relatively even competition. As in boxing, heavyweights competed against heavyweights. NASCAR arranged insurance, previously unavailable for tracks and competitors. Perhaps most important, NASCAR guaranteed the purses at the races it sanctioned. This rule was ironclad. In some cases NASCAR made promoters put their prize money in NASCAR's bank account a week before a race. A few times NASCAR had to dip into its own coffers to pay out the advertised prize money, and each time it did so, NASCAR strengthened its own reputation for being as good as its word.

In addition to guaranteeing the winners a just share of the proceeds at each event, NASCAR also initiated a national-standings system based upon points. The winner of a sanctioned race at a sanctioned track, whether it was in the Southeast, the West, or New England, would receive a set number of points. Lower finishers would receive points based on a descending scale. Promoters put 7 1/2 percent of their proceeds per race into the national points fund, and at the end of the season, the leading points winners in each automobile classification got the pot. By 1949 the national points fund contained $64,000. The awards were handed out in cash at an annual Victory Dinner, initially held at Daytona Beach. Now a black-tie affair at the swank Waldorf-Astoria Hotel in Manhattan, the annual awards dinner is the scene for distribution of a $2 million points fund, with an additional $1 million in cash awards.

There were early challenges to NASCAR's authority. The winner of the 1949 race at Charlotte, North Carolina, a major race on the circuit, was disqualified because of illegal wedges in the springs of his car. The owner sued. NASCAR won, legally establishing its right to set the rules at sanctioned races. NASCAR was not afraid to play hard-

ball with the drivers. When 13 racers decided to run at non-sanctioned tracks, France threatened them with loss of NASCAR national championship points. The racers drove at the outlaw tracks, and France took away their points. That was the end of the revolt.

But races were still being run at small, comparatively crude tracks. At the beginning of the Korean War, Indianapolis was the only superspeedway in the country, and it was available only to open-wheeled racers, a far cry from stock cars. Stock car racing could not compete with the Indianapolis 500 without a comparable race of national importance and a track to run it on.

Harold Brasington, a businessman and part-time racer from the small town of Darlington, South Carolina, had watched the annual Memorial Day race at Indianapolis and set out to build a rival speedway in his home town. His track would feature stock car racing. He sold stock in the venture to local residents, and when that money ran out, he offered stock to the laborers and suppliers who built the track. Begun in December 1949, the track was paved, a mile and a quarter long, banked at one end, and flat at the other. The Central States Racing Association won the sponsorship of the first race, but when it came up with only a half dozen entries, NASCAR stepped in and took over. Under NASCAR's sanction Darlington got off to a thundering start with a field of 75 racers and 30,000 paying spectators. The race was won by Johnny Mantz, driving a Plymouth coupe he had bought for $1,700 off the floor of a dealer in Winston-Salem, North Carolina, and driven to the track! His secret was a set of special racing tires that enabled him to drive the entire race at a moderate speed without stopping to change tires. It was a victory for "pure stock" and for NASCAR.

As its competitors dropped by the wayside, NASCAR became firmly established. NASCAR showed its power when Curtis Turner, a driver who was building the Charlotte Motor Speedway, approached the Teamsters Union for financial backing. Big Bill France suspended Turner until it became clear that the union would not be involved. Later, in 1969, driver Richard Petty—who had won a record 27 races in 1967 and was the leading spokesman for the sport—formed the Professional Drivers Association (PDA). Its stated purpose was to improve the pit road and garage-area conditions and assist drivers with endorsements. The

PDA's first action was to lead a boycott of the first race at Talladega in 1969 on the grounds that tires developed for that track were unproven. Some drivers also feared that the high speeds on the 33-degree banked, 2.66-mile super-speedway would generate heavy "g" forces that might cause them to black out. France ran the race with unknowns and, in effect, broke the union. A year later NASCAR, in a gesture that some saw as a compromise, introduced the carburetor restrictor plate to slow the cars down, improve safety, and foster more even competition.

NASCAR was able to survive the challenges because it was doing what it promised. Purses no longer flew by night but were actually growing, and the sport was expanding. In 1961 network television broadcast its first stock car race, the Firecracker 400 at Daytona Beach, on ABC's "Wide World of Sports." In 1963 Fred Lorenzen became the first driver to win over $100,000 in a single season. By 1971 Richard Petty became the first stock car racer with career earnings surpass $1 million.

Racing was also safer. The fuel cell, which greatly reduced the risk of fire in the car, became mandatory, and in 1966 Goodyear revolutionized tire safety with the unveiling of the inner-liner tire.

At the same time that Big Bill France was driving NASCAR to dominance, he was also planning the sport's biggest and fastest speedway. With a combined goal of moving local races off the beach and onto a Darlington-type paved speedway, France formed in 1955 the Daytona Beach Motor Speedway Corporation and encouraged the State of Florida to set up a Speedway Authority. Negotiations and financing plans took two full years, but by late 1957 construction was under way. France's corporation leased land from local governmental bodies for 50 years, with a 25-year renewal option. Financial backing came from Detroit automotive heir W.O. Briggs Jr., bandleader Paul Whiteman, Pepsi-Cola Bottling Company executive Don Kendall, Texas businessman and Dallas Cowboys owner Clint Murchison Jr., and the Lamar Life Insurance Company. Another big investor was Union Oil Company, which is why only Unocal 76 gasoline, the same you buy at the service station, is used in NASCAR races. The first race was a 500 miler on George Washington's birthday in 1959, won by Lee Petty.

The Daytona International Speedway is wildly suc-cessful. Speed Week, in February of each year, attracts hundreds of thousands of paying fans for a full week of racing, culminating in the Daytona 500, the World Series of stock car racing. The Firecracker 400, held on the Fourth of July weekend, draws large crowds, including in 1984 President Ronald Reagan, who gave the "Gentlemen, start your engines" command from Air Force One as he flew to the track.

In the late 1960s, France, now head of an expanded operation named the International Speedway Corporation (ISC), started construction of the Alabama International Motor Speedway. The 2.66-mile track at Talladega, Alabama, between Atlanta and Birmingham, was completed in 1969. The corporation acquired Darlington International Raceway in 1982, giving ISC control of three of the major stock car racing facilities. ISC also jointly owns the track at Watkins Glen, New York, with Corning Glass Works. International Speedway Corporation now has some 3,000 stockholders, and the stock is traded in the over-the-counter market.

In 1970 ISC added another jewel—Motor Racing Network (MRN). At the Daytona 500 that year, Big Bill France was unable to convince broadcasters covering the race to promote upcoming races, so he started his own broadcast network. Now MRN, with the familiar, knowledgeable voices of Barney Hall and Eli Gold, broadcasts the full Winston Cup schedule live on an average of 260 radio stations in 28 states, and the Daytona 500 goes worldwide through a link with the Armed Forces Network.

Because of the France family's involvement with both entities, it would be easy to confuse their relationship with NASCAR and ISC. The Frances own 100 percent of NASCAR, having bought out all minority stockholders by 1970. By contrast the France family holds approximately 48 percent of the stock in ISC, owner of the superspeedways at Daytona, Talladega, and Darlington and half owner of Watkins Glen. Additionally, the France family also owns, in its own name, 50 percent of the Martinsville (Virginia) Speedway.

While in many other businesses such interrelationships might bring charges of conflict of interest, observers agree that the France family is aboveboard. NASCAR treats all tracks even-handedly. The Daytona International Speedway, for example, pays the largest sanctioning fee to NASCAR of any track.

NASCAR is now a major business, employing more

Dick Beaty, Winston Cup Director.

than 75 full-time staffers in its comfortable and modern Daytona Beach headquarters adjoining the Daytona International Speedway and the Daytona airport. Its annual operating budget, estimated to be more than $5 million, is funded from membership dues and sanction fees paid by race tracks. NASCAR's membership roster has grown from one, Bill France, to over 30,000 drivers, pit crew members, owners, and fans. For $75 a year fans receive a newsletter, a jacket patch, and the pleasure of sharing membership with the biggest names in racing.

Perhaps symbolic of the coming of the modern era in racing, Big Bill France, with his roots in the dirt-track and beach-course racing of the 1930s, 1940s, and 1950s, resigned as president of NASCAR in 1972 and turned the reins over to his son William C. France, known as Bill Junior. While Big Bill is credited with bringing order from the chaos of the early days by organizing the points fund and ushering in the superspeedway era, Bill Junior is given high marks by competitors and fans alike for leading stock car racing from a regional to a national sport, with support from some of the world's largest corporations.

Under Bill Junior's leadership, NASCAR provides a number of services for the dollars paid by its members and tracks. It makes available the personnel that run the races. Under the firm but polite and even-handed direction of Les Richter, Vice President for Competition, Planning, and Development, and Winston Cup Director Dick Beaty, inspectors examine competing cars before and after each race. In the early years some competitors complained that NASCAR often acted in an arbitrary manner. Today, however, owners and drivers alike compliment Richter and Beaty for consulting with competitors before instituting rule changes and for discussing suspected infractions before imposing penalties. NASCAR also furnishes the timers and scorekeepers, who work under the exacting eye of Morris Metcalfe. A retired AT&T engineering executive, Metcalfe is leading the transition from a manual to a computerized scoring system. The flagman, Harold Kinder, and pace car drivers are all NASCAR-provided.

NASCAR continually reviews and modifies the rules, both for safety and to keep the sport competitive. When Bobby Allison's car blew a tire at 210 mph and went airborne at Talladega in 1987, NASCAR brought back the special carburetor restrictions at Daytona and Talladega to reduce speed. To keep stock car racing from suffering from the "rich get richer" syndrome, which has damaged other professional sports, NASCAR has recently imposed limits on the amount of costly private-track testing teams may do. Bill France warns, "Our biggest problem is cost, the cost of racing and keeping it in check."

Because post-race fines and suspensions proved ineffective in halting some rough driving by a few drivers, NASCAR instituted the "penalty box"—a driver is black-flagged off the track and sent behind the wall to cool off when flagrant rules violations are observed. It can be costly. Great drivers operating strong cars can often make up a loss of one or two laps, but even Dale Earnhardt could not regain the five laps that NASCAR penalized him for intentionally bumping Geoff Bodine at the 1988 World 600 at Charlotte. Earnhardt, who was in position to capture the $100,000 first prize before the penalty, could manage no better than thirteenth place, worth less than $20,000. "Peace and tranquility have to be restored," said France after the race. "We are going to see that it is, whatever it takes."

While most race fans smile at the notion of peace and

tranquility, they would agree when France comments, "What we want to see is good competition between all cars, and that's what the new rules have given us." Race fans know that races run at NASCAR tracks will, in the main, be safe.

Under the leadership of the France family, NASCAR/ Winston stock car racing has spread from the Southeast to the entire nation. Prize money has increased from small or no purses to the point where today's stars receive compensation packages equal to those paid stars in other professional sports. Races are run faster than ever, but in the well-constructed and thoroughly inspected Winston Cup cars, driver injuries are rare. In the safety-engineered grandstands, spectator injuries are almost nonexistent. In the well-policed, orderly crowds, all members of the family can attend and feel secure. Facilities and restrooms at most tracks are clean. "A fan has to enjoy the event," Bill France says. "He's there for recreation, and he doesn't want second-rate stuff." What once was the sport of Southern good ol' boys is now supported by an impressive roster of Fortune 500 companies and attended by their executives and families.

Like other major league organizations, NASCAR is becoming more actively involved in public service projects. A number of drivers have been publicly involved in anti-drug campaigns. Richard Petty, Neil Bonnet, Bobby Hillin Jr., and Darrell Waltrip have each filmed public service spots for television, and Waltrip has appeared with First Lady Nancy Reagan as part of her "Just Say No" campaign. NASCAR is working with the Department of Justice in its McGruff the Dog "Take a Bite out of Crime" promotion.

An unusual operation within NASCAR promotes money — big money — for somebody else. In order to foster competition by getting more sponsors to pour more money into more racing teams, NASCAR runs a well-oiled, aggressive marketing department under Jim Foster and his assistants, Bob Weeks and Kevin Camp. They have plenty to work with. Surveys show motorsports to be the fastest growing sports in the country. In contrast to the red-neck crowds of a generation ago, Foster's marketing research shows that half of the spectators at Winston Cup races earn more than $25,000 per year, and 20 percent earn more than $40,000. A third own three or more cars, and over two-thirds own their own home. Thirty-eight percent of the fans are women. And these demographics apply only to the tracks. Nearly every Winston Cup race is covered by television. Countless

people at home see those brightly colored cars roar by with the sponsors' names plainly visible at 200 miles per hour. The entire race is a commercial.

With such an audience, advertisers like Motorcraft, Quaker State, Miller High Life beer, and Levi Garrett Chewing Tobacco no longer have the field to themselves. Major advertisers now include the likes of Piedmont Airlines, Gatorade, Proctor & Gamble, Kodak, Union Carbide, Exxon, Southland Corporation, and Hardee's. Products typically purchased by women — Folgers Coffee, Crisco, Underalls, Tide, Coats & Clark thread — have also recently joined as sponsors of Winston Cup race teams.

"Our first priority," Foster says, "is to get them on the automobiles. If we don't have race cars that are well prepared, competitive, and look good, and if the teams don't have the money to have clean uniforms and look first class on the track, then we don't have a sport."

Once interested, a sponsor has several opportunities. A primary sponsor such as GM Goodwrench may invest upwards of $2 million to underwrite Dale Earnhardt's Chevrolet. Associate sponsorships of middle-ranked teams may involve a few hundred thousand dollars. Whatever the amount, NASCAR is eager to channel money into the under-financed teams to bring them closer to the front.

While ISC clearly is the dominant sponsor/track owner in stock car racing, many races are still promoted by independents like Paul Sawyer, owner of Richmond Fairgrounds Raceway Inc., which has put on two Winston Cup events each year for over 30 years, or Larry Carrier of Bristol International Speedway in Tennessee, which has operated that racetrack since 1960. In contrast to the ISC tracks, with races covered by live network television, accommodating 100,000 spectators, and paying a winner's purse of up to $200,000, the independent tracks are covered by regional or cable television, seat up to 60,000, and pay winner's purses of around $50,000. But these smaller tracks, with intensely loyal fans, still sell every ticket in the house, and because drivers get as many Winston Cup points for winning at Bristol as they do at Daytona, smaller tracks attract all of the top-ranked drivers.

Surprisingly, the smaller tracks have not gotten together to market a TV package that would ensure wider coverage and more even distribution of television revenues, as professional football has done since the 1960s. A few, such as Martinsville, one of the most attractive racing facilities with well-tended flower beds, clean restrooms, and accessible parking, do not permit TV coverage at all.

The so-called independent tracks are actually dependent for their very survival upon the whim and caprice of NASCAR, which grants its all-important sanction for only one year in advance. A promoter who wants to put millions of dollars into improving and expanding his facility, as Richmond's Paul Sawyer has done, does so at his own risk. Many knowledgeable observers foresee NASCAR races only in major media markets at longer tracks seating 100,000 or more. Promoters at smaller tracks consequently fear that they will suffer the fate of the Nashville track, which was dropped from the Winston Cup schedule. This can discourage them from investing in the very improvements, like upgraded restrooms, better parking, and expanded premium seating with corporate "sky boxes," that increase fan support.

As smaller tracks become endangered species, it is easy to see where their replacements will be. Just as Fortune 500 corporations have already been drawn into the sport, so may the larger population centers. Mega-markets such as Los Angeles and San Francisco, Dallas and Houston, New Orleans, St. Louis, and Chicago are currently without Winston Cup racing. Small tracks, hometown advertisers, and underfinanced owner/driver racing teams may someday become history.

But for the fan, the future of NASCAR racing looks bright. Sponsorships will grow in value. "Purses are good," says France, "but they can always be better." Within a few years, the Winston Cup championship could be worth $5 million. Corporations are getting sky boxes at many tracks to entertain VIPs. Winston Cup competition is certain to be expanded to major market tracks in New England, the Midwest, and Northern California. Races in Canada and Australia are viewed as a possibility. Yesterday one sandy beach—tomorrow the world!

RACE CAR

NOCAL **76**

True Val
Master ME

 Winston

SPEE
PRO PISTO
RINGS

BUSCH
Beer
Pole Award Winner

MICHIGAN
ENGINE BEARINGS

Goody's

MOOG
HIGH PERFORMANCE SUSPENSION PAR

Holley
CARBS

Auto
Meter
COMPETITION INSTRUMENTS

GOOD YEAR

BELTS & HOSE

PEAK
antifreeze & summer coolant

RRC

Gator

BIG MONEY

Stock cars are rolling commercials, and the 18-wheelers that carry them to the speedways are moving billboards. Drivers' uniforms are covered with sponsor logos. It is not subtle. Money drives this sport.

And it is *big* money. Sponsors spent almost $300 million on motor racing in 1987. The next biggest sports consumer of commercial dollars was golf, at $126 million.

You see much of that money whiz by on the cars themselves. Nearly every car has at least one major sponsor, whose name is plainly visible even at 200 miles per hour, and several associate sponsors, represented by smaller logos splashed over the car. Many sponsors offer special awards to drivers at individual races as well as cumulative, end-of-season awards. Major businesses also sponsor individual races and entire series of races. Heavy advertisers assign top-flight personnel to the program, year-round or for special events. Some pay their drivers $10,000 or more for a personal appearance. There are, in short, many ways to spend money in racing.

The money comes from many sources. Leading the pack is the R.J. Reynolds Tobacco Company, manufacturer of Winston cigarettes, and a subsidiary of RJR Nabisco Inc. Reynolds spends about $15 million each year on stock car racing. The enormous TV exposure alone is estimated to be worth $10 million in advertising value. Reynolds believes it's also smart business to provide the distinctive Winston red-and-white paint treatment at many tracks around the country, which will be seen by grandstand and TV fans alike, and to provide full-time personnel support to make things go smoothly.

Reynolds sponsors the Winston Cup Series of 29 races, the major league of stock car racing. The Winston Million is the sport's triple crown, presented to any driver who can win three of the biggest four races of the year. Bill Elliott picked up the award in 1985, along with his title "Million Dollar Bill." Reynolds sponsors the Winston 500 at Talladega and The Winston, a three-segment race run in Charlotte that pays the winner $200,000.

Winston also supports in large measure the minor leagues of stock car racing through several regional series and the national Winston Racing Series, run on some 70 tracks across the country. It includes several classes of cars: modified, pure stock, street stock, late model, dirt,

mini stock, limited sportsman, chargers, and pro stock.

Though these races reach drivers and fans in big and little towns all over America, nothing has the impact of the Winston Cup. Points, from a possible 185 for the winner on down, are awarded to every participant in each of the 29 races. The driver who accumulates the most points over the season wins the Winston Cup. Prize money goes not only to the top finishers at season's end, but also to the leaders at the mid-season point. The mid-season leader gets a $150,000 check, scaling down to $10,000 for the tenth-place winner. At a black-tie dinner at New York's Waldorf-Astoria Hotel at season's end, the overall winner, who could, of course, already have picked up the mid-season check, gets $400,000, second place $225,000, and on down to $20,000 for twentieth place.

Other sponsors tie additional awards, totaling over $1 million, to the Winston Cup points championship, all presented with fanfare. Unocal 76 pays $100,000 to the season's leader. Donors include Busch; Champion; Gatorade; Goody's; Sears, Roebuck & Company; Stewart-Warner; Stokely-Van Camp; STP Corporation; True Value; and TRW.

With all this, a Winston Cup points champion can receive close to $1 million in one night, on top of purses earned during the racing season. The top drivers today—Earnhardt, Waltrip, Elliott, and Wallace—can expect to earn about $2 million in a championship season.

Another season-long sponsor is Anheuser-Busch Companies Inc., whose Busch beer sponsors the Grand National Series, the training ground for Winston Cup drivers, with purses of $200,000 or more. It also presents awards to Busch pole winners and runners-up in the qualifying runs. The brewing company sponsors four Winston Cup races: three Budweisers at Dover, Riverside, and Watkins Glen, and the Busch 500 at Bristol.

Unocal Corporation, whose Unocal 76 gasoline powers all NASCAR events, and Goodyear, whose tires are on most cars, invest over $1 million each in awards. Quaker Oats Company, owner of Gatorade Thirst Quencher, puts up several hundred thousand dollars each year to have the winning driver at each race gulp down a few swallows of its drink right out of the bottle while sitting in Victory Lane.

NASCAR administers one of the biggest pools of

money available to car owners, the Winners Circle program. Race promoters contribute a portion of their gate receipts to this fund, which pays almost $200,000 to each of the top 11 teams each year. A team "on the Winners Circle" receives the cash award only if it enters, passes inspection, and attempts to qualify at each of the 29 Winston Cup races. A single unexcused default costs the team its entire share of the Winners Circle award. While the program has been criticized by some as helping the rich get richer, it does enable race promoters to advertise that all of the biggest name drivers and teams will be present at each race, helping to guarantee a sold-out event.

Most of the 29 major league races are title-sponsored, at costs running from $50,000 to $500,000. In 1988 these races were the Goodwrench 500, Motorcraft 500, Valleydale Meats 500, First Union 400, Pannill Sweatshirts 500, Winston 500, The Winston, Coca-Cola 600, Budweiser 500, Talladega/Diehard 500, Budweiser 400, Miller High Life 500, Miller American 400, Pepsi Firecracker 400, Budweiser At The Glen, Champion Spark Plug 400, Busch 500, Miller High Life 400, Goody's 500, Holly Farms 400, Oakwood Homes 500, AC-Delco 500, Checker 500, and the Atlanta Journal 500.

Some observers might note that the first race of the season, the Daytona 500, does not carry the name of a sponsor. Though major industries have bid as high as $500,000, Big Bill France has chosen to turn down outside money and call the race simply the Daytona 500. The Southern 500 at Darlington, a Labor Day weekend tradition, also remains sponsorless.

To the owners of the race teams who put the cars on the tracks, the important money is that which flows directly to the cars themselves. Some receive upwards of $2 million a year in the form of sponsorships. Traditionally, sponsor money has come from tobacco companies such as U.S. Tobacco Company's Copenhagen Snuff and Skoal Bandit, Levi Garrett, Kodiak, and Helme Tobacco Company's Chattanooga Chew; beer like Coors, Budweiser, and Miller High Life; and automotive suppliers such as Ford's Motorcraft Parts, GM's Mr. Goodwrench, Gunk Liquid Wrench, TRW's DiGard, Ashland Oil Company's Valvoline Oil, Nationwide Auto Parts, Alugard Antifreeze, and Zerex Antifreeze.

But today's sponsors, aware that 38 percent of those who attend Winston Cup events are female, are no longer limited to producers of "masculine" products. More and more cars advertise household products—Tide laundry de-

tergent, Lifebuoy soap, Coats & Clark thread. Cooking and food products like Crisco, Folgers Coffee, Bull's-Eye Barbecue Sauce, Citrus Hill orange juice, Kentucky Fried Chicken, and Holly Farms Chicken are prominent; women's and children's clothing such as Underalls pantyhose, Bull Frog Knits, and Pannill Knitting can be seen; and Slender You Figure Salons are also visible sponsors.

Advertisers are convinced that they get their money's worth. Sponsor's Report, a marketing industry service that records the number of minutes and seconds each race car is clearly shown on the television screen during the course of a race, determines the commercial equivalent value of such exposure for its clients. Following Winston cigarette's $10 million worth of television exposure are Budweiser and Busch beers, which receive more than $7 million of exposure for an annual investment of some $4 million. The recipient of one of the best return-on-investments is thought to be STP Corporation, which is reported to spend less than $2 million per year sponsoring Richard Petty's Pontiacs while receiving almost $6 million of commercial exposure! Figures such as these have drawn more Fortune 500 companies like Eastman Kodak Company, Piedmont Airlines, and Exxon Corporation into car sponsorships.

For companies who do not want to support an entire car, contingency sponsorships are available. A car displaying the sponsor's decal on its front quarter-panel receives a prize of anywhere from a few hundred to a few thousand dollars for finishing among the top five. Many cars display 15 or 20 such decals—for Simpson Helmets, STP Oil Treatment, Monroe Shock Absorbers, Bilstein Shock Absorbers. Awards like these can increase the posted promoter's purse by as much as $10,000 a race.

Many other sponsors pay a basic administrative fee of $6,000 per year, plus a minimum of $1,000 per race, to paste decals advertising their products on the front fenders of the race cars. The decal of one company, Pro-Cal Racing Decals, advertises decals. A winning driver who displays, for example, a Champion Spark Plug decal and certifies that he used that product in the race, receives $1,000 from Champion. Companies ranging in size from Sears (Diehard batteries) and Unocal (gasoline, lubricants) to Monroe (shock absorbers) and Simpson (racing helmets) participate as "contingency award sponsors."

Perhaps the most dramatic proof of what NASCAR sponsorship can do for a product came at mid-season in 1988, when Lever Brothers Company's Lifebuoy soap, in its ninety-fifth year, came out in a handsome new wrapper. As reported by Larry Edsall, motorsports editor of *Auto Week*, the marketing event had its beginnings not in a Madison Avenue advertising conference but at the Firecracker 400 at Daytona in 1987. Dave Marcis, in the Lifebuoy car Number 71, finished a good third. While receiving congratulations, he laughed and said that he could have won if only he'd been driving a blue car.

Thanks to his sponsor Lifebuoy, Dave got his wish for the 1988 season, a beautiful blue car with light-blue and white stripes. The car and its affable driver made such a hit with the fans that Lever Brothers got the message. They repackaged their soap in the colors of the new race car. Instead of the car reflecting the sponsor's product-packaging, the product-packaging resembles the car!

Sponsors for NASCAR Winston Cup stock car racing include: AC-Delco Spark Plugs, AEX Equipment, Allen Glass, All Pro, Almeda Auto Parks, Alugard Antifreeze, Amer-Flint Paint, American Home, Amoco Oil, Anheuser-Busch, A.R.P. Automotive Fasteners, *Atlanta Journal*, Auto Meter Instruments, Baby Ruth, Banks Oil Company, Banquet Frozen Foods, Bell Helmets, BCR Crankshafts, Bilstein Shocks, Bowmalloy, Budweiser, Busch, Busch Polishes, Bull Frog Knits, Bull's-Eye Barbecue Sauce, B & W Auto Supply, BW Race Cars, Caerte Engines, Carlite Auto Safety Glass, Castle Hi-tech, Champion Spark Plugs, Chattanooga Chew, Checker, Citgo, Citrus Hill, Coats & Clark, Coca-Cola, Coleman Disc Brakes, Competition Cams, Coors, Copenhagen Snuff, Country Time Lemonade, Crane Cams & Rockers, Crisco, Crown, Curb Records, Delco, Delco Batteries, Delco-Remy, Detroit Gaskets, Desina-Rec, Dixon Steel, Earl's Performance Products, Earl's Plumbing, Earl's Supply, Edelbrock Manifolds, Eureka Vacuum Cleaners, Explorer Vans, Exxon, Exxon Motor Oils, Fel-Pro Gaskets, First Union, Folgers Coffee, Food Lion, Frederick Chevrolet, Gatorade Thirst Quencher, Gilmore Copenhagen, GM Goodwrench, Go Jo, Goodyear Hoses, Goody's Headache Powders, Griffin Radiators, Gunk Liquid Wrench, Hardee's, Havoline Motor Oil, Heinz Ketchup, Helen Rae, Hempstead Abstract & Title Company, Holley Carburetors, Holly Farms Chicken, Howard Stewart Valves, Hummin' Bird, Ingersoll-Rand Tools, Inmont Products, Instant Oil Change, JE Pistons, JFZ Disc Brakes, Joseph Lang Co., Kentucky Fried Chicken, Kmart, K & N Filters, Kodak Film & Paper, Kodiak, Kroger Stores, J. Omar Landis Enterprises, Levi Garrett, Lifebuoy, Linro Racing, Loctite-Permatex, Mac Tools, Matco Tools, McCord Gaskets, Melling Auto Products, Metro Mobile Telephone, Michigan Engine Bearings, Miles Concrete, Miller High Life, Mobil Oil, Modine Radiators, Monroe Shocks, Moog Chassis Parts, Moroso Oil Pans, Motorcraft Ford, Motor Sports Designs, Mr. Gasket, MSD Ignitions, National Motors, Nationwide Auto Parts, Newton's Collision, Oakwood Homes, Oberg Filters, Oldsmobile, Oliver Billet, Packard Electric, Pannill Sweatshirts, Peak Antifreeze & Coolant, Peddler, Pepsi, Perfect Circle Valve Stem Seals, Piedmont Airlines, Plasti-Coat Paint, Poly Dyn Polishes, Pontiac, Port-A-Lube, Pro-Cal Racing Decals, Purolator Filters, Quaker State, Quarter Master, Race Car Engineer, Red Baron Frozen Pizza, Reed Carburetors, Research Labs Inc., Richmond Gear, Rods & Mains, Rubenton Construction, Rumple Furniture Company, S & H Racing, Saginaw, Schoenfield Headers, Sears Diehard Batteries, T.G. Sheppard, Simpson Helmets, Skoal Bandit, Skoal Classic, Slender You Figure Salons, Snap-On Tools, Solar, Solder Seal, Solder Seal-Gunk, Sony Magnetic Products, Southern Biscuit, Speed-Pro Piston Rings, Stant Radiator Caps, Stewart-Warner Instruments, Van Camp's Pork and Beans, STP Oil Treatment & Oil Filters, Stratagraph Inc., Stroh Light, Sunoco Ultra Products, Superior Piping, Texaco, Thermo Dynamic, Tide, Tilton Clutches, True Value Hardware, TRW Automotive, Underalls, Unocal 76 Oil & Gasoline, Valleydale Meats, Valvoline, VHT, Victor Oil Seals, Volyes Auto Salvage, Wayne Paging, Webster Radiator, Wehrs Chevrolet, Wilder Nuts & Bolts, Wiseco Pistons, Winston, Wrangler, Wynn's, and Zerex Antifreeze.

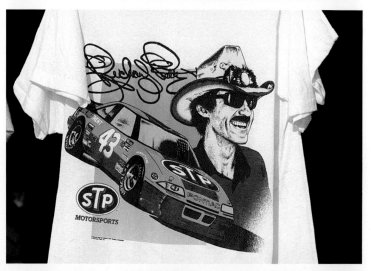

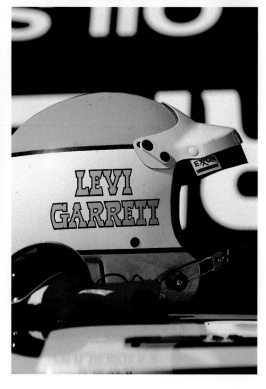

ACKNOWLEDGMENTS

NASCAR. Jim Hunter, NASCAR Vice President, himself the author of several books on racing, provided initial encouragement and continuing assistance. He read and commented extensively upon the manuscript. Jim Foster, NASCAR Vice President, spent several hours (in person and via long-distance telephone) explaining the inner workings of NASCAR, including explanations of the relationships among the France family, NASCAR, and International Speedway Corporation; Jim also read and commented upon the manuscript. Les Richter, NASCAR Vice President, talked me through a race from the NASCAR tower and explained the technical inspection process to me. He also read the manuscript. Bob Weeks, NASCAR Director of Sponsor Services, spent literally hundreds of hours digging up information for me and helping me open doors to drivers, team owners, and track officials. Bob read the manuscript. Morris Metcalf, Chief Scorer, spent an afternoon explaining the elaborate race scoring system to me. Dick Beaty permitted me to sit in several owner/driver meetings and answered questions about the rules in a lengthy telephone interview. Lisa Horn and Nancy Wilhite of the NASCAR staff assisted in making arrangements for my visits to Daytona and in many other ways. I am indebted to each of them for their patience and help.

Track Officials. The officials of many tracks extended courtesies to me. I am particularly grateful to W.D. "Red" Tyler Jr., President of Darlington International Speedway; his capable secretary, Clarice Lane; and Woodrow M. McKay, General Manager, for their hospitality (and access) at the 1986 Southern 500. One of the most attractive facilities on the Winston Cup circuit is Martinsville Speedway, and H. Clay Earles, Clay Campbell, and Dick Thompson provided hospitality to me on a number of occasions. At Daytona International Speedway, Larry Balewski and others made visits to Speed Weeks in 1987 and 1988 pleasant and productive. At Richmond Fairgrounds Raceway — now the newest and always one of the most exciting places to watch a race — Paul Sawyer (for whom I have unbounded admiration for his continuing contributions to improvements in racing) and Kenneth Campbell have provided courtesies before and during several races.

Team Owners. The entire Hendrick Motorsports operation, which owns the Waltrip/Tide/Chevrolet, the Bodine/Levi Garrett/ Chevrolet, and the Schrader/Folgers/Chevrolet, has been of tremendous assistance. I hope my admiration for everyone connected with those organizations has not clouded my objectivity in the text. Rick Hendrick, a successful businessman, dedicated sportsman, and visionary, has spent a great deal of time discussing the future of Winston Cup racing with me. His assistant, Steve Matchett — a talented photographer, race driving instructor, and one of the most thoughtful and articulate people in the sport — spent many hours explaining fine points of driving and racing to me and very kindly read the manuscript for errors. Jimmy Johnson, the accountant-turned-race-team-manager, not only has helped me to understand the finances of the sport (though I hasten to add he did not comment upon published reports about salaries paid to his employees), but he also spent an afternoon giving me the guided tour of his teams' facilities. Waddell Wilson spent several hours showing me the basics of engine building, and Gary Nelson helped explain car building. Likewise, the Junior Johnson organization was courteous and helpful. Junior spent a morning in September 1987 taking me through his shops and giving me his evaluations of many Winston Cup drivers; Bob Latford, public relations representative for Johnson's sponsor Anheuser-Busch and one of those who has made numerous contributions to the development of racing, has given freely of his time at the race track, at Junior's shops, and over the telephone. He, too, reviewed and commented upon the manuscript. Richard Childress, owner of the Earnhardt/Goodwrench/Chevrolet, also gave me a personal tour of his state-of-the-art facilities in Welcome, North Carolina, and spent several hours (in Welcome and at Talladega and Richmond) talking racing with me. He permitted me to stand in his pit during the 1987 Talladega 500 and took the time to explain race strategy to me. Childress's engine builder, Lou LaRosa, showed me how he builds the engines that almost never fail. I greatly appreciated their efforts to make this a good book.

Drivers. The following drivers gave me lengthy personal interviews: Alan Kulwicki, Bill Elliott, Bobby Hillin Jr., Terry Labonte, Benny Parsons, Ricky Rudd, Rusty Wallace, Darrell Waltrip, Cale Yarborough, Sterling Marlin, Geoff Bodine, and Rick Wilson. The other drivers whose mini-biographies appear here were willing to grant interviews, but because of scheduling difficulties, they were unable to spend any extended time with me. Each driver was sent a copy of the manuscript and asked to correct factual inaccuracies; the following either telephoned or mailed comments: Kulwicki, Earnhardt (who indicated through his wife Teresa and a spokesman, Tom Kincaid, that he liked almost nothing that I wrote about him), Elliott (through his able public relations aide, Alexis Leras), Hillin, Labonte (through Bob Latford of the Junior Johnson/Anheuser-Busch team), Kyle Petty (through his agent, Don Light), Richard Petty, Rudd, Wallace, Waltrip, Yarborough, Marlin, Geoff Bodine, Wilson, and Schrader. Each of these drivers has an exceptionally demanding schedule, and I deeply appreciate the amount of time they gave me.

Press. Ned Jarrett, who is a two-time Winston Cup Champion, ESPN sportscaster, and father of up-and-coming driver Dale Jarrett, spent a generous amount of time checking the manuscript for errors. Steve Waid, executive editor of Grand National Scene — the tabloid racing weekly devoted to Winston Cup and Busch Grand National racing exclusively — also read and commented upon the manuscript. I owe a particular debt to Steve's many, many articles — written well and thoughtfully under the unrelenting pressure of deadline — in Grand National Scene and Grand National Illustrated, for giving me valuable background and factual information about racing.